EASY A
MO[N

A detailed guide to some of the most beautiful ascents in the Mont-Blanc massif for the beginner mountaineer (routes graded "Easy" to "Slightly Difficult"). Includes the basic theoretical and technical knowledge necessary before setting out into high mountains: gear, skills, safety, route-finding. Invaluable tips and advice from professional mountaineers.

François BURNIER
Dominique POTARD
Mountain Guides

Translation and adaptation:
Brian Rawcliffe and **Nicole Lehmann**

Le Vieux Servoz - 74310 SERVOZ - FRANCE

By the same authors:
- Guide des écoles d'escalade de la vallée de Chamonix ,1989, reprinted 1996, new edition 2001
- Escalades en Espagne/ Climbing in Spain, 1990 (Out of print)
- Mont-Blanc: courses faciles, 1993
- Chamonix hors-pistes/ off piste, 1995
- Thaïlande, escalades/ Rock-climbing, 1995
- Crag climbs in Chamonix, 1998, new edition 2001

All our thanks to:
Jacques BERNY, Isabelle GAUTIER, Elisabeth HAZA, Florence LASSERRE, Jean-Pierre MANSART, Marco MINOGGIO, Geraldine MONZO, Xavier MURILLO, Nathalie POTARD-FEUTRY, Didier POUDEROUX, and the P.G.H.M. in Chamonix.

Cover photo: Xavier MURILLO

Printed in Italy

© Copyright Editions **VAMOS, 2002**
www.editionsvamos.com

Printed by MARCOZ s.n.c., Place E. Chanoux, 1
11017 Morgex, Italy- Tel. (0039) 01.65.80.96.40

All translation and reproduction rights reserved in all countries.
Drawings by Dominique POTARD.

I.S.B.N.: 2-910672-09-3, 4ème édition revue et corrigée; dépôt légal: juillet 2000
I.S.B.N.: 2-910672-05-0, 3ème édition revue et corrigée; dépôt légal: juin 1997
I.S.B.N.: 2-9503673-8-0, 2ème édition revue et corrigée; dépôt légal: juin 1993
I.S.B.N.: 2-9503673-2-1, 1ère édition sous le titre "Du Buet au Mont-Blanc".

FOREWORD

This guidebook's ambition is to help all mountain lovers (hikers, climbers and adventurers of all kinds) to discover the possibilities offered to them in the Chamonix Valley and start making their dreams come true.

It is divided into three parts:
- Part one containing a basic introduction to the techniques of mountaineering.
- Part two minutely describing ten easy ascents, classified in increasing order of difficulty.
- Part three dealing with ten more difficult ascents, also classified according to levels of difficulty.

These ascents are situated in the Mont-Blanc and Aiguilles-Rouges ranges, a natural paradise in which mountaineering was born and developed. We wish this guide will be an instructive and reassuring climbing companion. **However, it may in no way be considered a substitute for the services of an instructor or a mountain guide. High mountains are an extremely dangerous environment.**

If you are a beginner, this guide will help you select the routes which are the most appealing to you and improve your understanding of what the guide expects from you or what a certain ascent implies. When you are a confirmed alpinist and go out on your own, on a route you have perhaps done before with a guide, this book will be of great use. But should it happen one day that after a bend on a ridge or a glacier, our explanations seem senseless, what is to be done? All mountaineers have had to confront this dilemma at least once!

Stop, close the book, look around very carefully, and ask yourself: "If I happened to be the first person to ever have come here, which way would I go?". And your own common sense will often give you the right answer.

A mountain-guide in the Chamonix valley, Francois BURNIER is also a Physical Education teacher and an Economics graduate. Born in Haute-Savoie, he has rock-climbed from an early age and to a high level, and it was quite natural for him to become a mountain-guide after completing his university education.

Dominique POTARD is a guide and ski-instructor in the Mont-Blanc massif, where he has climbed more than 500 routes. He has worked as a technical advisor at the U.C.P.A. He holds a University Diploma in Tourism from the University of Savoie. He is also a novel writer and a cartoonist.

Section 1

AN INTRODUCTION TO THE TECHNICAL ASPECTS OF MOUNTAINEERING

- Is it necessary to hire a guide? . . . . p. 8
- Some vocabulary . . . . p. 10
- Equipment and gear . . . . p. 12
- Techniques and safety . . . . p. 16
  - Environmental dangers
  - Route-finding in the mountain
  - Effort at high altitudes
  - Methods of progression
- About the weather . . . . p. 28
- What to do in the event of an accident . . . . p. 29
- Mountain-huts . . . . p. 32
- Choosing an ascent and finding information . . . . . p. 34
- Knowing when to turn back . . . . p. 37

The following pages will allow you to have a better understanding of the different technical aspects of mountaineering: use of equipment, choice and preparation of a route, movement on different terrain (snow, ice, rock). The question is: "How to develop an awareness of what mountaineering involves?" It is obvious that such a complex environment as the high mountains cannot be reduced to a few pages of explanation! Our modest ambition here is only to provide some information on the issues at stake and clues for a correct understanding of the route descriptions which follow.

Becoming a mountaineer is a long apprenticeship. It is not simply the challenge of mastering yet another physical skill, but also a question of coming to terms with a natural, often hostile, environment. It is this second aspect which takes the most time to acquire and which is very difficult to describe in books. That is why it seems important to us to begin with considering the role of the mountain-guide, a mythical figure of those higher spheres and a the link between the mountain and the world "below".

IS IT NECESSARY TO HIRE A GUIDE?

All beginners start off asking themselves this question. The cost of hiring a guide, often felt to be high, does not always encourage an answer in the affirmative. The general philosophy underlying our guidebooks is that mountaineering is first of all a human adventure, an experience to be lived through but also learnt from. So, we would be tempted to reply: "Yes, but intelligently, with discernment, and not necessarily at all times".

"Yes", because even the best and most specialised books cannot replace a practical view of things. Because your team-mate who knows "quite a bit about it" might not be able to pass on to you the fruits of years of experience in the way a professional guide might.

"Intelligently", in the choice of which way you are going to use the services of a mountain-guide. You can hire a guide for a specific route, alone or with a friend or two; but you can also attend a course or a session, individually or as part of a group. If you are a beginner, for example, a course is a good way to learn.

"With discernment" in your choice of an ascent. Do not aim too high, as your guide will probably be able to get you to the summit but you would not enjoy it. You must also try to have an intelligent relationship with your guide: ask him questions, observe his way of doing things, particularly in the route-finding business. Beware, however: his expertise allows him to take liberties that you might not be able to take for quite some time, such as moving together on tricky terrain or using minimal protection on pitches.

"Not in a systematic way", although we do think that the traditional climbing party of the client and "his" guide is a very happy way of touring the mountains (where the client, lacking any expertise, wouldn't dream of venturing out into the mountains alone). But we consider that every mountaineer should strive to become responsible and self-reliant. The time spent climbing with a guide can thus be seen as a learning experience which will allow him one day to tackle the "great adventure" in a safer way.

To begin with a guide, to attempt to put into practice, on your own and on modest objectives, what you have learnt, then regularly to meet up again with a professional to learn the next stage, is the way to give yourself a good chance of succeeding.

Important contacts:

- Compagnie des Guides de Chamonix: Tel 04.50.53.00.88
- Association Internationale des Guides du Mont-Blanc: Tel 04.50.53.27.05
- Bureau des Guides d'Argentière: Tel 04.50.54.00.12
- Bureau des Guides de Vallorcine: Tel 04.50.54.60.71
- Bureau des Guides de Servoz: Tel 04.50.47.21.68
- Bureau des Guides des Houches: Tel 04.50.54.50.76
- U.C.P.A. Centre, Argentière (collective sessions only): Tel 04.50.54.07.11

SOME VOCABULARY:

Abseil : lowering oneself on a rope.

Ascender : (or camming unit) mechanical device allowing one to go up a rope.

Balling up : term used for snow that sticks in a compact ball under the skis or crampons and make them less efficient.

Belaying : protecting by holding the rope as one goes up or down a tricky section.

Bergschrund : large crevasse on the side of a glacier between the moving glacier and the solid bank.

Cairn : heap of stones made up by alpinists to mark the top of a mountain or to outline a trail.

Carabiner : metal snap link which ropes or slings are clipped into.

Chocks/ friends : pieces of metal mounted on loops of wire which can be wedged into cracks and used as protection.

Cornice : overhang of snow over the top of a ridge, made by the action of the wind.

Couloir : gully or passage between two rock-walls or rock-faces.

Crevasse : deep crack formed on a glacier by the action of the ice moving downhill.

Figure 8 : one type of device commonly used for belaying.

Gendarme : prominent rock tower standing isolated on a ridge. The word means policeman.

Gondola : lift-system with several or many small units rather than one big cable-car.

Leading/leader : the first on the rope, or most experienced member of the party.

Locking carabiner : carabiner with a screwgate or other locking gate, much safer for belaying.

Moraine : steep slopes of earth and rocks carved out by a glacier or mounds of earth and rocks transported by a glacier.

Névé : permanent snow in the mountain.

Quickdraw : device commonly used for belaying on rock-climbs, made up of two carabiners connected by a small tape-sling.

Ridge / arête : more or less angled part of a mountain separating two slopes. A very long ridge at the top of a range is called a crest. The crest line is a succession of crests outlining the horizon, joining several peaks and mountains.

Rognon : means kidney and is used for a small rocky blob or outcrop. There exists such a word as kidney-stone in English but mountaineers use the French word.

Roped party/rope : group of people linked with a rope for greater safety on a glacier or a ridge, or a steep snowy slope, usually 2 or 3 members.

Scree slopes : slopes covered with small loose stones, uneasy to walk on.

Serac : ice blocks forming a chaotic mass at breaking points in the glacier.

Serac-fall : unpredictable and deadly glacial activity due to the slow motion of the glacier. The only way to avoid them is to pass quickly and be lucky.

Sling : loop of flat tape used for belaying (e.g. on rock-spikes) and carried slantwise across the chest..

Windslab : compact snowpack formed on the leeward side of a slope, and very liable to breach and avalanche.

THE EQUIPMENT

Having the right equipment is essential for your own safety and comfort. Take special care over the choice of boots, which, on their own, can turn an enjoyable ascent into a nightmare.

1. **RUCKSACK**: Neither too big nor too small (around 40/45 litres capacity). It should have a flexible frame, be cylindrical and taller than it is wide, with not too many "gadgets" such as pockets or straps of all kinds which only serve to catch in cracks or fissures!

2. **HARNESS**: Shown in the photo is a sit-harness mostly used in rock-climbing. For mountaineering, a full body harness (sit-harness plus chest-harness) is thought to be safer, as the weight of a rucksack alters your balance and you may end up hanging upside-down, which is dangerous if lengthy (in a crevasse for example).

3. **CRAMPONS**: Twelve points. Several reliable methods of attachment exist; "quick fit" crampons are generally more expensive, but considerably simplify the putting on and taking off sessions.

4. **BOOTS**: Plastic shell boots with a separate inner are ideal for long snow routes, but less convenient than leather boots on rock, as these are more supple (but less waterproof...). A good fit is essential: search for just the right size.

5. **JACKET**: Ideally, it is made of a fabric which is both windproof and waterproof. The traditional "duvet" has been replaced by modern waterproof/breathable fabrics such as "Gore-Tex". Underneath , wear polar fleece or wool rather than cotton or down. Several thin layers are better than one thick one, as their number can be regulated according to the temperature.

6. **HELMET**: Lightweight, but conforming to European safety standards.

Photo: François BURNIER

7. **SLINGS (TAPE LOOPS or ROPE LOOPS)**: Take at least 9mm rope, or 25mm flat tape loops. Tape is convenient and lightweight, but more liable to damage through abrasion. It should be inspected frequently for signs of wear.

8. **BELAY DEVICE (FIGURE 8 OR BELAY PLATE)**: Used for rappelling or belaying (protecting) a companion who is lead-climbing.

9. **ICE SCREWS**: conical, tubular or corkscrew (these don't work too well, but are perfect for opening bottles!) The tubular ones are the most reliable.

10. **TROUSERS**: Like the jacket, windproof and waterproof. For purists, breeches will guarantee you the old fashioned style (not too efficient in bad weather though...).

11. **ICE-AXE:** Metal shaft and toothed pick. Not too short- unless you intend to climb the odd icefall. For a 5 foot 9 inches mountaineer (approx. 1m75), a 75 - 80 cm axe should be right.

12. **CARABINERS:** Screwgate or other locking-carabiners are essential (unless you use two non-locking carabiners with gates opposed and reversed). Take 4 locking-carabiners per person. The photo shows two sets of carabiners connected by a small tape loop. They are called "quickdraws" and are needed for ascents involving serious rock-climbing. 10 to12 per party will be sufficient for all the routes described in this book.

13. **CHOCKS:** Pieces of metal hung on small wire or rope loops, used for wedging into cracks in the rock, to act as protection points. Easy to place and remove. They come in various shapes and sizes.

14. **FRIEND/STOPPER:** It is a sophisticated mechanical chock which will fit into a range of widths of cracks, even "flared" ones. Also comes in various sizes. Very expensive.

15. **ROPE:** For the routes described here, a "single" rope of 10,2 to 11mm diameter, about 40 m long, will do. Rappel ropes (8,5mm diameter) are used double and measure 70 to 100 metres.

...and to complete the outfit:

- **MAPS:** see references below.

- **COMPASS AND ALTIMETER, OR G.P.S:** they can't be dispensed with. Make sure you are proficient with your G.P.S. before you throw away your old compass.

- **HEADTORCH:** check the batteries before leaving the valley.

- **GAITERS:** they go between trousers and boots when you walk in the snow and stop your boots turning into an aquarium!

- **GLASSES:** good-quality sunglasses for pure rock routes, glacier glasses (much darker) for snow routes.

- **GLOVES:** light and warm (polar fleece or leather) plus a warmer pair for early mornings. Avoid mittens, they are clumsy.

- **HATS:** both woollen hat and sun hat/cap may be necessary in one day.

- **SUNSCREEN:** take the subject seriously. Don't forget earflaps or the back of your neck.

TECHNIQUES AND SAFETY

Travelling in absolute safety in the mountains is impossible, because the high-mountain environment is uncertain and unpredictable by nature. Risk can be kept to a minimum by a combination of technical and environmental knowledge, physical and mental stamina, skills and ability.

ENVIRONMENTAL DANGERS

In high places, the environment itself involves hazards which are called "objective". You should become familiar with them and try and develop habits and routines which will tend to reduce the risk of accidents.

LOOSE ROCK

Rock-fall may be due to temperature variations, which dislodge stones, or to the clumsiness of climbers above you.

Advice:
- Avoid lingering in couloirs and gullies, which are natural collectors for stone fall, or at the foot of steep rock faces.
- Make your presence known to climbers above you.
- Wear a helmet.
- In the event of rock-fall, quickly find natural shelter or protect yourself with your rucksack.

FALLING SERACS

A result of glacial activity, they are totally unpredictable and may occur day and night.

Advice:
- Look uphill and identify the seracs presenting risks.
- Avoid passing below seracs whenever possible. When you can't avoid it, pass quickly through the danger area.

CORNICES

Formed by the action of wind and snow on ridges. They are a danger to parties climbing below them, as well as to those actually on the ridge.

Advice:
- Do not expose yourself to cornice danger when the sun is hot.
- On a corniced ridge, make your track lower down.

AVALANCHE
Above 3500 meters, precipitation generally falls as snow or hail, even in summer, so there is always an avalanche danger after a period of bad weather.
Advice:
- After bad weather, find out about the extent of the snowfall and about the direction of the wind, so as to identify the slopes where snow may have accumulated in the form of windslab. Take an Avalanche Tranceiver/ beeper and a snow shovel.

LIGHTNING
It is common in summer, towards the end of the afternoon.
Advice:
- Clouds on the summits, getting bigger through the day (cumulonimbus), can be a sign of a storm to come.
- Plan early ascents and stick to your schedule, so that you are off the route early, between noon and 2.00 p.m.
- Check the weather forecast just before you start.
- If caught in a thunderstorm, don't panic, as you run the risk of making a mistake. "Make haste slowly", as the saying goes, to an area less exposed to lightning (a ledge, a glacier, below a summit).

STORMS
Bad weather can last for several hours to several days, and change a quiet ascent into a nightmare.
Advice:
- If you become lost in a storm, stop and wait for an improvement.
- Find shelter instead of wandering around in the storm. Look for natural shelter (rocks, blocked up crevasse) or build a snow shelter (snow provides very good insulation).
- Keep a survival blanket, a small stove to heat water, and some emergency food in the bottom of your rucksack.

ROUTE-FINDING IN THE MOUNTAIN

After many years of hiking in the mountains, route-finding will become like a sixth sense. Be very wary at the beginning.

THE MAP
- 90% of the time the map alone will be enough for your navigation.
- Always carry a 1:25000 map of the climbing area.
- Use your map as often as possible during the climb.
- To locate your position, identify the neighbouring summits.
- Learn to read the map: identify valleys, hills, the angle of a slope, etc.
- Plan your ascent route meticulously, on the map.

THE COMPASS AND ALTIMETER OR THE GPS
- The compass indicates the magnetic north. It allows you to define precisely the general direction you want to take.
- The altimeter indicates the altitude you are at. It is also a barometer, as it varies according to the atmospheric pressure, so that altitude measurements are not always reliable in case of a sudden change in the weather (pressure going up or down).
- Together, they are vital instruments in bad weather... provided you use them correctly!
- The G.P.S. is a decisive step in navigation techniques. It has brought about much more safety. Some are specifically designed for mountaineering use.
- To learn more about navigation techniques, you must refer to books dealing specifically with the subject.

EFFORT AT HIGH ALTITUDES

High altitude, heat, wind and cold will put a great strain on a human body unaccustomed to them. They may even badly put it to the test. You should therefore know about the effects of high altitudes, so that you can assess your physical capacity in a realistic manner.

ALTITUDE

Shortage of breath, headaches and vertigo are quite normal signs of the effects of altitude on a non-acclimatised person. They are due to a reduced air pressure (at the top of Mont-Blanc it is about half that at sea level), and to rarefied air (it contains less oxygen).

However, if during a night in a mountain-hut, your headache cannot be cured by aspirin, if you feel out of breath even when lying down, or suffer a loss of balance, these may be the early symptoms of altitude oedema (fairly rare in the Alps). In this case, only one solution: go down immediately.

Acclimatisation occurs after about 6 days in high places. The body then produces more red corpuscles so that the blood can carry enough oxygen, even in low air-pressure.

Nearly half of the people who attempt the ascent of Mont-Blanc do not reach the summit because of a lack of preparation at altitude. So when you plan to complete a route over 4000 meters, it is essential to get acclimatised by completing several training routes at a lower altitude in the days before.

COLD:

During a summer day, temperature variations can range over as much as 30 degrees Centigrade. Temperatures of -10°C to -5°C are fairly common in early mornings.

Advice:
- Choose good quality gloves, boots and hat.
- Wear good wind protection, as the wind aggravates the effect of the cold.

HEAT AND SUNRAYS

In mountaineering, the effort needed is long and intense, in extreme conditions of heat and solar radiation.

Advice:
- Drink a lot to avoid dehydration, which will bring about cramps and tiredness. Snowmelt is drinkable, but don't drink it when still icy.

METHODS OF PROGRESSION

Moving neatly on slippery, unstable and dangerous terrain, wearing big boots and crampons, is not easy. Mountaineering is like learning to walk again.

SNOW AND ICE

Glaciers are the terrain on which the beginner mountaineer will spend most time. They are usually covered in snow, a very unpredictable element. Its consistency varies according to its depth, its temperature, the orientation of the slope and the time of the day. The climbing party will have to adapt to the snow conditions in order to progress safely.

Ice appears mostly on the lower parts of a glacier, or on the summit slopes of a mountain.

Although walking on a glacier which is not covered by snow could seem very unfriendly at first, its advantage is that crevasses are seen... so, no surprises. On the other hand, climbing an ice slope, even one which is not very steep, calls on skills a novice mountaineer may not have acquired yet.

WHEN TO USE CRAMPONS?

Crampons should be put on your boots with care. If well adjusted, they should stay on the boots without the straps.

On snow:
- Use them when the snow is frozen and hard (often the case in the early morning).
- Use them in moderately hard snow if you haven't yet "found your feet" as a mountaineer.
- In soft snow, they are not necessary.
- If the snow "balls up", that is, if it sticks to the underside of your crampons, forming a ball of snow, tap your crampons with your ice-axe. To help prevent this inconvenience, anti-balling plates are usually optional with most crampons. They are an important "plus" for safety.

On ice:
- Crampons are always necessary, except on the flat parts of uncrevassed glaciers.

ASCENDING
- On slopes of up to 40 degrees, progression is made by zigzagging up the slope, taking small steps and remaining well in balance... Remember this when you are tempted to take long strides to get off that tricky section as quickly as possible!
- On steeper ground, climb facing the slope.
- Hold your ice-axe as a walking stick, in your uphill hand, with the pick forward. It is used for balance, not as something to cling to!

When wearing crampons, stick to these four rules:
1. All the points should bite into the ice (flex your ankles).
2. Take small steps.
3. Keep your feet well apart, so as not to stick the points into your trousers (wide trousers, such as tracksuit bottoms are unsuitable).
4. Stamp your feet, so that the points will dig into the ice.

GOING DOWN
It is harder to master than ascending.
- Go down facing out.
- Stamp your heels in, keeping your body well in balance, knees bent, pelvis pushed forward.

GLISSADING
On uniform snow slopes, it is possible to slide on your boots (without crampons!), using the ice-axe for support (fig. 1). It is a useful, fun method, which makes the descent easier. Avoid using it on slopes situated above rock faces...

GOING DOWN STEEP SLOPES
- walk down backwards, facing into the slope, using the front points of your crampons;
- use a rope set up as a "handrail";
- use a top rope (with figure of 8 or other belaying device) or rappel slings (abseil).

CHECKING A FALL
If you slip, you must slow your fall, so as to reduce the effort needed by your climbing partner to hold you on the rope. It is important to react quickly. This calls for experience and practise.

Two examples of possible reaction:
- get into the glissade position (only if you are not wearing crampons);
- get onto your stomach (if wearing crampons, keep your feet clear of the snow, otherwise... goodbye ankles!), and press down firmly on the pick of your ice-axe to slow yourself down, but don't try to "plant" the axe in the snow (fig. 2).

JUMPING A CREVASSE:
If, as is often the case, you must jump over a crevasse, assess its width, not its depth. Jump with or without a run up, but with determination, taking off as close to the lip of the crevasse as possible.

STEEPER ICE SLOPES
Even on an easy route, you may come across a few metres of very steep ice. In that case you must "front point", that is, dig in only the front points of your crampons.

Advice:
- imagine that you are climbing a ladder, with your weight on your feet;
- keep your legs well apart, to remain in balance;
- keep your heels low, with your calf muscles relaxed;
- plant your axe firmly, as high as possible.

Fig. 1 : Glissading

Fig. 2 : Checking a fall on snow

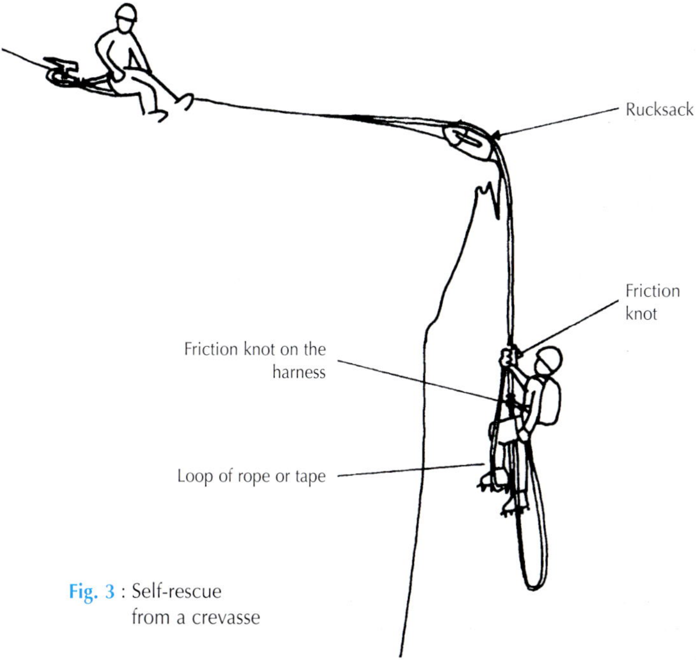

Rucksack

Friction knot

Friction knot on the harness

Loop of rope or tape

Fig. 3 : Self-rescue from a crevasse

MOVING AS A ROPED PARTY

In mountaineering, the rope is used as a precautionary measure. It is the link which will save your partner in the event of a slip, or if a snow bridge gives way under his feet. Rope management calls for precision and concentration, especially when beginning.

A roped party generally consists of 2 to 3 people.

Tying on:
- tie on to your harness with a figure 8 knot (fig. 4), following the instructions given by the harness manufacturer;
- make loops around your chest with the excess rope. Tie them off with an overhand knot. Before fastening it, pass the loop behind the chest loops and into the tie-in point.

PERSONAL EQUIPMENT:

In order to be able to cope with a possible crevasse rescue, each mountaineer must carry a certain amount of equipment hanging permanently on his or her harness:
- two loops of 5 mm cord, 50 cm long, to be used to make friction knots, also called Klemheist knots or Machard knots (fig. 6);
- one loop of rope or flat tape, 1,50 m long;
- one locking carabiner;
- two ordinary carabiners;
- two ice-screws;

Note: 2 mechanical ascenders can replace the friction knots.

The rescue techniques will be described in a further section.

THE ROPED PARTY ON THE GLACIER

Keep a distance of 10 to 15 metres between each member of the party. Walk with the rope kept fairly tight so that if someone falls into a crevasse, the sudden pull on the other person will be weaker.

About 20 cm from your tying-in point, make a small overhand loop in the rope for rescue purposes.

Keep covered up! Never walk bare-armed or in shorts on a glacier: falling into a crevasse is always a possibility.

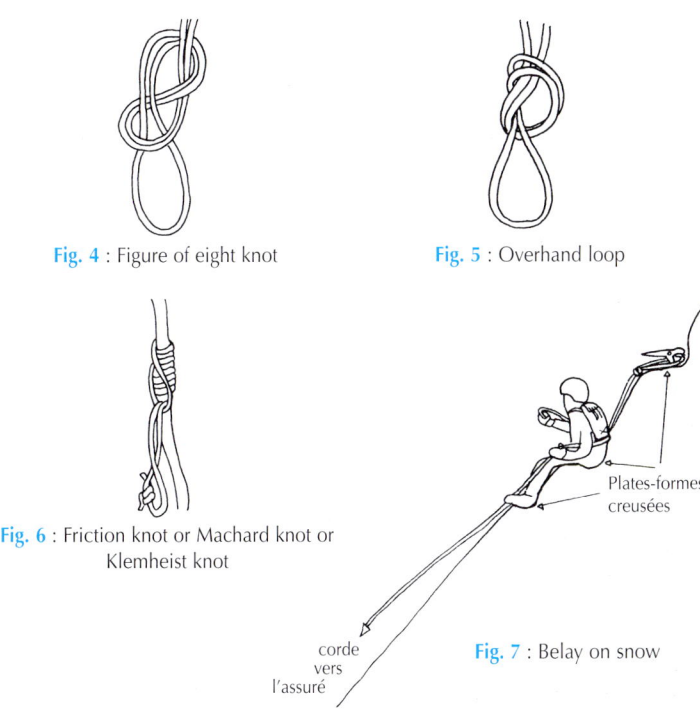

Fig. 4 : Figure of eight knot

Fig. 5 : Overhand loop

Fig. 6 : Friction knot or Machard knot or Klemheist knot

Plates-formes creusées

corde vers l'assuré

Fig. 7 : Belay on snow

THE ROPED PARTY ON MEDIUM SLOPES (up to 40° angle)

When leaving the glacier to climb the snow slope to a summit, the risk presented by crevasses disappears. The rope then serves to prevent a further fall in case someone slips.

The distance between members of the party should be reduced to 2 to 3 metres. The first on the rope (the most experienced member of the party) keeps a few loops of the rope in his hand. He must be able to check a sudden fall of his partner at any time.

THE ROPED PARTY ON STEEP SECTIONS

Even on a route graded Easy or Slightly Difficult, a steep section, such as a bergschrund, may be encountered. In that case, climb in "pitches", that is, climb the section one after the other.

First, a belay is taken on an ice-axe (if the snow permits) or on an ice-screw (if the section is on ice). The second should attach himself to the anchor point, using an overhand loop, and belay the leader using a waist belay, sitting down with his back to the slope and well supported by his feet.

On reaching the top of the tricky section, the leader belays the second as he climbs up. (fig. 7).

THE ROPED PARTY ON A RIDGE

The distance between members of a party on a snow ridge should be around 3 metres:
- If the ridge is ascending, the leader should be in front, carrying several loops of the rope in his hand.
- If the ridge is descending or horizontal, the leader should be behind.
- In the case of the second slipping down one side of the ridge, the leader should let go of the loops and jump down the other side - this calls for quite a bit of practising!

RESCUE FROM A CREVASSE

On a glacier, the risk of a fall into a crevasse exists at all times and must be faced with a cool head. It can be quite inconsequential, if the party is properly tied-up.

Depending on the case:
- If the glacier is busy, call for help and pull the victim out.
- If there are three of you, one keeps hold of the rope, the other helps the victim, taking care to belay himself.
- If you are alone, the victim will have to use self-rescue techniques. Several methods exist. We shall explain the most widespread method, using friction knots (Klemheist knots).

SELF-RESCUE USING FRICTION KNOTS (fig. 3)
The person holding the rope:
1. Anchor the rope solidly, either on the ice-axe if snow conditions permit, or on ice-screws if the ice is accessible. To do so, use the overhand loop you had previously made 20 cm from your tying-in knot.
2. Untie, and place a rucksack or piece of clothing under the rope, on the lip of the crevasse, so that it does not cut into the snow.

The person climbing out:
1. Put both friction knots on the rope, about 80 cm apart (the knots are made from the two 7 mm cord-loops you carry on your harness).
2. Attach your harness to the lower friction knot using a locking carabiner. This attachment should be very short.
3. Attach the large loop made from the 1,50 metre loop of rope or flat tape (you carry it around your chest) to the upper friction knot. Step up on it. Push the lower friction knot up the rope. Both friction knots are then moved alternately up the rope.

Advice: Practise knot-making and go over the whole thing many times before you take the risk of falling into a crevasse!

ROCK
The rock sections on the routes described in this book do not necessitate any specific formal training. They are within any good hiker's reach.
Basic climbing hints:
- Take small steps. Use a succession of small holds, rather than a large step.
- Don't pull yourself up on your arms.

THE ROPED PARTY ON ROCK
The party will move together on easy routes, with 2 to 3 metres between members of the party. On ridge routes, extend the distance to 10 or 15 metres, taking care to zigzag between rock spikes, so that the rope will jam behind the rock in the event of a slip. On vertical sections, climb in pitches, that is, one at a time, the first on the rope belaying the second from the top.

ABOUT THE WEATHER

It is generally believed that the weather is not too good in the Chamonix Valley. It has even been said that it rains a lot... which is undoubtedly rather excessive. But it is true that the height of the Mont-Blanc massif does not really allow the clouds to go their way undisturbed!

For the mountaineer, the vital point is to become aware of any bad weather to come. Here are a few tips:
- Bad weather generally comes from the west.
- It can occur very quickly. It is not unusual for a storm to break over your head less than two hours after a clear blue sky.
- The most characteristic warning sign is the presence of lens-shaped clouds on the summits of Mont-Blanc and Aiguille Verte. The locals call them "ânes" (asses), from "bonnet d'âne" (dunce's cap).

The local saying is "Ce que Verte veut, le Mont-Blanc ne peut" (What the Aiguille Verte wants, the Mont-Blanc can't avoid). It means that if the cloud is only over Mont-Blanc, bad weather is not certain, but if both mountains are capped... take out your umbrellas!

If a long period of bad weather is forecast, a good alternative is to go through the Mont-Blanc tunnel to the Gran Paradiso massif. Less than a two-hour drive away from Chamonix, it has superb, easily accessible ascents at altitudes approaching 4000 meters, often with better weather conditions. However, this is only the case when the bad weather comes from the west and not from the south.

- Weather information
- Telephone "Chamonix Météo", (33) 08.92.68.02.74. For climbers. Two to three specific bulletins a day, on an answering machine.
- Minitel 36.15, code METEO.
- http://www.meteo.fr, OR www.chamonix.com
- Display outside "la Maison de la Montagne" in Chamonix, and at the Tourist office in Argentière.

WHAT TO DO IN THE EVENT OF AN ACCIDENT?

The three basic rules taught in first aid courses for organising help in the case of an accident are equally valid in the mountains: **PROTECT, ALERT, ASSIST**.

- **PROTECT**: it means keeping the victim away from any further injury, sheltered from stone fall, in a place where they do not risk slipping and belayed as securely as possible, warm, etc, (not necessarily by moving the victim).

- **ALERT**: before starting on your ascent, memorise the number for mountain rescue (PGHM) on your mobile phone: 04.50.53.16.89. If the zone is not well covered or if you don't own a mobile phone, see below for the conventional distress signals. One is rarely completely isolated in the Mont-Blanc Massif.
The problem now is to try and attract the attention of other mountaineers, without panicking, and explain to them, as clearly as possible, what happened. They will alert the rescue services and will be able to give them the maximum amount of information. The effectiveness of the rescue will be increased by the following information: what is the nature of the injuries? Is a doctor's presence necessary? What equipment are the rescuers likely to need?
If you have to raise the alarm yourself, first look to the physical and mental security of the victim, who needs explanations and reassurance. Accurately note and signal the position of the victim, particularly in a crevasse, (make a large circle in the snow, surround the crevasse with visible, solidly anchored equipment). Be quick but not rash, as it has been shown that many accidents happen to people trying to call for rescue (fall into a crevasse, slip). Whatever the case, your main purpose must remain not to aggravate the situation. Don't try desperate actions, but contrive to act with cool logic, even if it is not easy when you are in an emotional state. The places where the alert can be raised most efficiently are the mountain-huts and the lift-system. On the Mont-Blanc route, there is a radio beacon in the Vallot Hut.

- **ASSIST**: if you stay with the casualty while another party raises the alarm, you can administer first aid. Again, don't make any rash decision but restrict yourself to safe and necessary actions. Above all, avoid moving your team mate if there is any risk of injury to the spine.

The rescue service will probably arrive by helicopter. The best way to help them is to position yourself so that you are easily visible, with the wind behind you, and your arms raised in a "V". You can also help the pilot spot you by laying out a conspicuous piece of material, anchoring it with stones. Spotting mountaineers from a helicopter is not easy: the massif is extensive and during the summer, there are many climbing parties about. If necessary, wave your waterproof or anorak to attract attention. You should previously have taken care to tie down any loose objects, which could fly away in the down-draught from the rotor blades. While the helicopter is approaching, keep kneeling and move as little as possible. Always approach a helicopter from the front, so as to remain in the pilot's field of vision. Wait for a signal before you approach and duck your head. Rotor blades can take an angle and sweep down very unexpectedly at any time, especially in case of wind.

From then on, you must trust the rescuers completely: they are outstanding specialists. Alerting the rescue services is a serious action. Only an accident that you can absolutely not deal with justifies implementing such an operation, which is often dangerous for the rescuers themselves.

Important: There should always be someone in the valley who knows where you are and when you should be back. The "Office de Haute Montagne" can fulfil this role (address below).

DISTRESS SIGNALS

Stand up straight, both arms raised, stay still

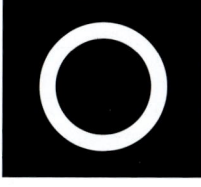

Red cloth, one metre square, with a white circle

Red distress flare, very effective, especially at night. On sale in specialised sports shops

WE NEED HELP

Stand up straight, one arm raised, motionless

WE DON'T NEED ANYTHING

Mountain-rescue: "Peloton de Gendarmerie de Haute Montagne" (P.G.H.M.): **04.50.53.16.89** / Emergency: **18** or **112** from a mobile phone.

MOUNTAIN-HUTS

You will find listed below the huts serving the routes described in this book. They all have a warden in the summer season, that is, someone who maintains the place, offers cooked meals and oversees life in the hut. That is the person to ask about what time to get up in the morning, for the ascent you intend to climb. He or she may also take an active part in ensuring the safety of mountaineers, for example by enquiring about parties who have gone out but not returned.

To make life easier for everybody in the hut, it is important to respect the warden's rules: to store ice-axes and crampons in the assigned place, not to wear big boots inside (you will find slippers to wear around the hut), to respect the set times for lights-out and silence. Other mountaineers may have ambitious projects and may need to get up very early in the night. It is essential for them to be able to rest for a few hours. Finally, take care to take all your rubbish back down to the valley with you.

All this may seem a little too strict and inflexible, and not compatible with the image of freedom associated with the mountains. In fact, as in any place where people live communally, the atmosphere in the hut will be warm and friendly if everyone respects everyone else.

Here is what you can expect to find in a mountain hut with a warden: mattresses, blankets, bar, cooked meals, a room for cooking on your own gas-stove. It is strongly recommended to take a sheet sleeping bag with you, for hygiene and personal comfort.

Important: Always reserve your bed by telephoning the hut the day before, at the latest. For the Goûter Hut, reservations have to be made several months beforehand!

- **Refuge de Pierre-à-Bérard (1950 m)**: private, 40 beds.
  Open and wardened all summer. Tel 04.50.54.62.08

- **Bivouac du Petit Mont-Blanc (3047 m):** private, 8 beds. No warden.

- **Refuge Albert 1er (2706 m):** Club Alpin Français, 130 beds.
  Wardened all summer. Very popular. Tel 04.50.54.06.20

- **Refuge de Tré-La-Tête (1970 m):** private, 80 beds.
  Open and wardened all summer. Tel 04.50.47.01.68

- **Refuge d'Argentière (2771 m):** Club Alpin Français, 140 beds.
  wardened all summer. Tel 04.50.53.16.92

- **Refuge du Requin (2516 m):** Club Alpin Français, 80 beds.
  Wardened all summer. Tel 04.50.53.16.96

- **Refuge du Plan de l'Aiguille (2203 m):** private, about 50 beds.
  Wardened all summer. No telephone.

- **Refuge des Cosmiques (3600 m):** 04.50.54.40.16

- **Refuge des Conscrits (2703 m):** Club Alpin Français, about 60 beds.
  Wardened all summer. 04.79.89.09.03

- **Refuge du Goûter (3817 m):** Club Alpin Français, 80 beds.
  Wardened all summer. Tel 04.50.54.40.93
  Make reservations as early as possible.

CHOICE OF ASCENTS AND INFORMATION

Twenty routes have been selected for this guide-book. They have been ordered systematically according to their difficulty but also in a pedagogical sequence. Our purpose is that each route should introduce a new aspect of mountaineering in a way which will help you understand it. We would therefore advise a novice mountaineer to try and follow this progression. However, it is obvious that this is only a theoretical approach and that other deciding factors should be taken into account, such as the state of the mountain, the season and the weather, your own physical condition and the time at your disposal.

So, we advise you to read carefully the introductory passages to each of the routes. We hope they will help you choose according to your ability and taste. Once having made the choice of a route, it is important to find as much current information as possible about it, and especially if it is "in condition". What does that mean? It means that mountains are an ever changing environment: glaciers move down, drought or heavy rain considerably alter rock faces, snowfall brings the risk of avalanche, early mornings, if not cold enough, bring stonefall dangers, and so on.

For example, for a snow route to be "in condition", there should have been no recent heavy snowfall, and the weather forecast should predict an early morning frost (0 degrees centigrade below the start of the route.)

Clearly, such information cannot by provided by a book. In Chamonix, it is a privilege to have the means of providing mountaineers with such information, with the Office de Haute-Montagne "Gérard Devouassoux" (address below).

There are many more routes, other than those described here, which are worth a visit. Each time, before going on the route, try to get all the information you can. The famous mountaineer, Louis LACHENAL, used to say: "When an ascent is well planned, it is already half completed".

SOURCES OF INFORMATION
- ***Office de Haute-Montagne:***
   Address: Place de l'église, Chamonix. Tel 04.50.53.22.08. Open all the year round. You will find all the information you need for route planning: conditions, mountain-huts, route descriptions, etc.
   The office is an unusual and very useful creation of the Chamonix City Council. Its mission is to contribute towards a safer access to the mountains through information and prevention.
   Do take the time to drop in there, you will be met with a friendly welcome by very competent staff.

- ***Books:***
  - **The "Vallot" guides** are technical books describing all the routes in the Mont-Blanc massif, the result of huge amounts of work. They are exhaustive but of rather austere reading and they contain very basic descriptions for the easy routes.
    For a long time considered as the "bible" for mountaineers, these high quality works are now out of print. Arthaud Publishing Company have published a new edition of these guides, which unfortunately has not retained what was one of the major qualities of the previous one: its detail.
    On the other hand, they are made easier to understand thanks to very precise photographs. The original edition can be found at the "Office de Haute-Montagne".

  - **The Mont-Blanc Massif, the 100 finest route**s, by Gaston Rébuffat (new edition in French, Denoël, 1995; first edition in English by Kaye and Ward, 1975). A magnificent book which has already kindled many a mountaineer's imagination.
    Beautiful photographs and great text. Some route descriptions are rather brief, perhaps to leave more room for adventure?

- **The "Piola" Guidebooks**. Excellent books, with a modern presentation, well suited to the experienced mountaineer.
- **Sommets du Mont-Blanc**, by J.L. Laroche and Florence Lelong, (Editions Glénat). An interesting selection of ascents, with good route descriptions (brush up your French before setting out).

- *Maps:*

L'Institut Géographique National (I.G.N.) covers the massif in two maps, 1:25.000 (1 cm = 250 m). Excellent.

On a larger scale, you will find the "Mt Blanc-Beaufortain" map, edited by Didier et Richard, equally well made (1:50.000).

KNOWING WHEN TO TURN BACK

In his book "Les cent plus belles" (The 100 finest routes), the famous alpinist Gaston RÉBUFFAT expressed this central question in those terms:
(Assessing the situation requires...)
"an extraordinary and rewarding inner analysis, in the secret depths of each person's heart, where prudence could just be one aspect of cowardice, and a valiant refusal to turn back just a stubborn and dangerous distortion of will."
In order to know when to turn back, you must be able to consider the situation with a clear head, and perhaps to accept the fact that the route is too difficult for you, that the conditions are not good, or that far too much time has already been wasted.

Being able to give up when necessary is an act of wisdom. Fortunately, mountaineering doesn't boil down to a frantic pursuit of summits, with the success of your plans as the only source of pleasure.

Being a mountaineer is being in the mountains, sitting on a granite boulder, walking along the lip of a crevasse or travelling along some snowy ridge. Being a mountaineer is knowing how to stay alive in the mountains.

No mountain is worth the loss of a human life.

Section two

A SELECTION OF TEN "EASY" ROUTES

1. Le Buet . . . . p. 42

2. Le Moulin de la Mer de Glace . . . . p. 44

3. Le Petit Mont-Blanc . . . . p. 46

4. L'Aiguille de Toule . . . . p. 48

5. L'Aiguille des Grands Montets . . . . p. 52

6. La Tête Blanche . . . . p. 56

7. La Bérangère . . . . p. 59

8. La Glière . . . . p. 61

9. Le Col du Tour Noir . . . . p. 64

10. L'Aiguille du Tour . . . . p. 68

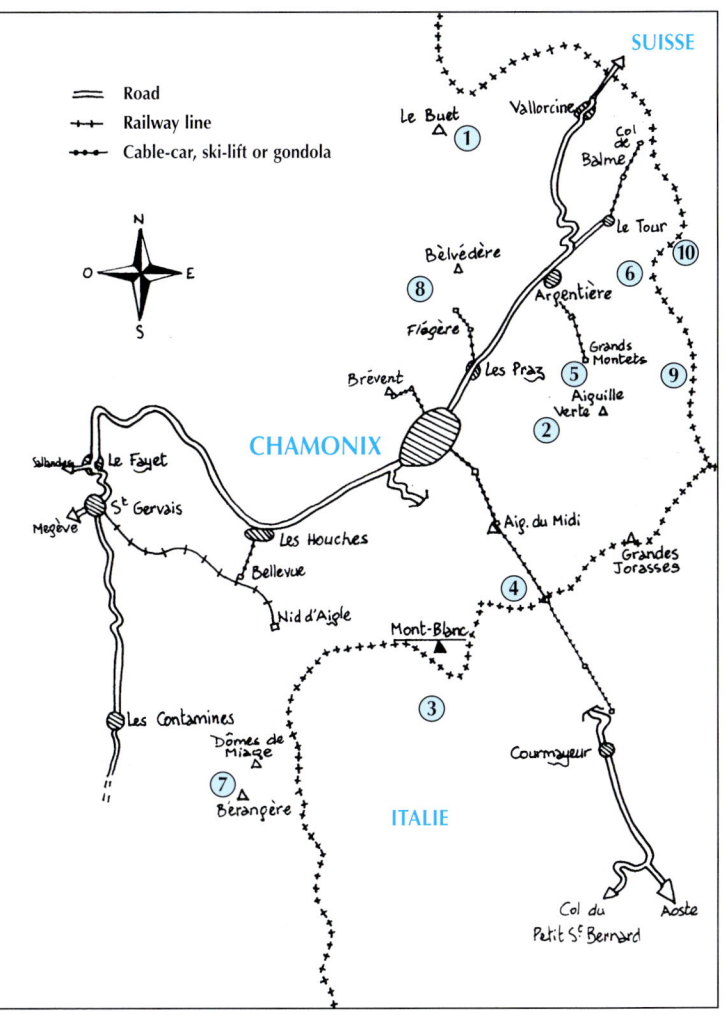

LE BUET (3096 m)

Some mountains somehow seem to sit in exactly the right place, and to raise their noses just high enough to overlook all the surrounding scenery.
Le Buet, also known as "Le Mont-Blanc des Dames" (ladies' Mont-Blanc), is one of those, and the extensive panorama unfolding as you climb is one of the most prestigious views in the Alps.
Its ascent does not present much difficulty and it is a good way for a reasonably fit walker to get in some training for more strenuous adventures. However, the route calls for stamina, especially if you plan to complete it in one day. We recommend a stop over at the small Pierre à Bérard Hut, to adjust smoothly to the swing of high mountain ascents.
Keep your eyes open for chamois and ibex: they have a soft spot for this beautiful mountain.

Difficulty : several steep sections require a certain amount of care and the track is not always well marked. We would advise you to tackle this ascent only when the weather conditions are quite reliable.

Vertical climb : 600 m to the hut, 1750 m in total.

Time : 6h (including 2h to the hut).

Suitable period : mid July to October.

Equipment : good mountain boots, warm clothing, gloves, sun glasses, possibly an ice-axe.

Map : I.G.N. TOP 25 3630 OT CHAMONIX.
Swiss map: 1344 Col de Balme.

- **Route**: from Chamonix take the road to Switzerland and go over the Col des Montets to the hamlet of Le Buet (railway station). From there, take a good track climbing to the Pierre à Bérard Hut through a lovely little valley, with some beautiful waterfalls.
  The hut is open and wardened all summer - make reservations the day before at the latest. Telephone: 04.50.54.62.08.

Ibex on the slopes of Le Buet / Photo: Jacques BERNY

From the hut, follow a steep track in a north-westerly direction until you stand below the Salenton pass (about 3 h from the hut). Then head north on a track skirting round the Aiguille de Salenton, then joining and climbing the slopes coming down from the Mortine arête (there may be some hard snow at).
The Mortine arête is a wide ridge, snowy but not too steep leading easily to the summit.

- **Descente**: follow the same route in reverse.

LE MOULIN DE LA MER DE GLACE (2050 m)

The Moulin de la Mer de Glace (the mill of the ice-sea) is an interesting and unusual goal and provides a good opportunity for a walk on this mythical glacier. It is a gigantic pit, regularly hollowed out by the snowmelt from the Mer de Glace, as explained by Louis REYNAUD, glaciologist at the CNRS: "...on a glacier, at the foot of a serac fall, there is a compression zone (i.e. no crevasses). There, trickles of water due to the summer thaw merge, forming a "bédière" (torrent) which flows on the surface of the glacier until it reaches a crevasse. At this point, the water plunges down and cuts out a chasm. To begin with, it is only about 20 metres deep, but very quickly, with the thermal and mechanical action of the water, it deepens and continues its way through rifts of great depths..." (translated from "Montagnes Magazine" number 89).
It was explored for the first time in 1898 by Joseph VALLOT and M. FONTAINE, using ladders, to a depth of sixty metres!
Later, in 1986, a team led by Jean-Marc BOIVIN, actually reached 110 m.
As far as mountaineering is concerned, the Mer de Glace does not present any major difficulty, but it does require suitable equipment. Don't play the fool, like so many tourists each summer, who venture onto the glacier in shorts and trainers!

Difficulty : Easy (F)
Time : 1h30.
Suitable period : from July to October.
Equipment : ice-axe, crampons, rope, harness, gloves, glacier glasses, warm clothing.
Access : from Chamonix, take the cable-railway (mountain railway) to the Montenvers station (1909 m).
Map : IGN TOP25 3630 OT CHAMONIX

- **Route**: From the top station, don't take the gondola but follow a wide track going down to the Mer de Glace ice cave. Leave this track 100 m after the first big left-hand bend for a track on the right leading to a series of vertical metal ladders climbing down.

Once you have set foot on the glacial moraine, you can easily reach the edge of the glacier. The track used nowadays is about 100 m lower than the original track, now impassable due to rockfall.

Put on your equipment for glacier travel, and heading towards the south-east, reach the middle of the glacier. Climb up the central section, keeping slightly to your left and crossing a series of crevasses, towards the medial moraine. Follow this to an area with fewer crevasses. When reaching the level of the ladders leading to the Envers des Aiguilles Hut - marked by an obvious square of paint - look for the "mill" (moulin) using the noise of the waterfall (bédière) as a guide. (1h30)

The Mer de Glace and the Moulin with the Grandes Jorasses in the background.

Photo: François BURNIER

LE PETIT MONT-BLANC (3424 m)
Normal Route

The Val Veny borders the Italian side of Mont-Blanc. There are no resorts, no cable-cars, but beautiful larch forests and picture postcard meadows. It is one of those remote alpine paradises where nature is still intact.

The summit of the Petit Mont-Blanc looms up quickly as you climb up Val Veny. It does remind one of its big brother, although it is only one minor peak in the chain that leads to the Aiguille de Tré-la-Tête. The ascent can be divided into three sections. It begins with a wide track winding up an alpine meadow and overlooking the Combal lakes. Then it climbs a long steep gully to reach the Petit Mont-Blanc bivouac hut. The ascent ends with a snowy ridge.

First ascent:
G. Bobba, Cosinur Herisod, Maurice Bognier 4th September 1897

Difficulty	: Easy (F): the fairly lengthy vertical ascent requires a certain degree of fitness. When climbing the gully, take care to stay on the track: a good exercise for route-finding practise. Early in the summer season, it may help to put on crampons to climb the gully.
Dénivelé	: 1350 m.
Time	: from the Lac de Miage snack-bar to the bivouac hut: 3 to 4 hours. From the bivouac to the summit: 1h to 1h30.
Equipment	: ice-axe, crampons, rope, helmet advisable.
Suitable period	: from July to October.
Map	: I.G.N. TOP 25 3531 ET. SAINT-GERVAIS
Access	: go to Italy through the Mont-Blanc tunnel. When you reach the small village of La Saxe, at the entrance to Courmayeur, turn right towards Val Veny. Follow the road until it becomes unsuitable for motor vehicles. Continue on foot to the Lac de Miage snack-bar.

- **Route**: Follow a good track, marked in red, leaving from the snack-bar. First, the track crosses an alpine meadow. Then, after a short section of easy climbing, it disappears into a gorge (between the small peaks of Combal and Mont Suc).

  From there on, take care to follow the track which at times loses itself in the scree. When the gully widens out, after crossing some easy rock slabs, head left to a small pass (altitude 2800 m) close to the Aiguille de Combal.

  Climb a series of rocky steps on the right of the pass, to reach the Petit Mont-Blanc bivouac.

  From there, reach the summit by climbing the snowy ridge (1h30 from the bivouac hut).

- **Descent**: follow the same route in reverse.

AIGUILLE DE TOULE (3535 m)
East Ridge (Normal Route)

The Aiguille de Toule used to be called La Ronde (the round one). "Toule" means "meadow" in the local dialect. This ascent can be seen as a short training route, but it would be wrong to believe it is of secondary interest.
First of all, it is set in exceptional surroundings, on the French-Italian frontier ridge, with an extraordinary view over the south-west slopes of Mont-Blanc, a fantastic wall on an almost Himalayan scale.
Secondly this route will allow you to test your "puff" at altitude, without too much commitment because of its close proximity to the cable-car.
Finally the route is varied: glaciated terrain followed by a short snow slope, and finally a rib composed of broken rocks.
Moreover, the Vallée Blanche gondola makes the approach "walk" very comfortable and it is worth a visit in itself: an eerie trip over a white immensity, which makes you forget instantly the justified controversy over excessive development in the high mountains.

First ascent:
10th August 1895 by *G. Robba* and *L. Vaccarone* with the guides *Casimir Thérisod* and *Pierre Re-Fiorentin*.

Difficulty : Easy (F). The rocky steps of the ridge, which can be loose in places, should be treated with care.
Height : 150 m vertical ascent between 3400 m and 3534 m.
Time : about an hour's climb at a slow pace.
Suitable period : June, July, August, September.
Equipment : ice-axe, crampons (can often be dispensed with), gloves, sunglasses, rope, harness, warm clothing.
Map : I.G.N. TOP 25 3630 OT CHAMONIX.

On the Summit of the Aiguille de Toule
Photo: Dominique POTARD

- **Approach**: completely mechanical!... From Chamonix take both stages of the cable-car to the summit of the Aiguille du Midi, then the Vallée Blanche gondola to Pointe Helbronner (about an hour's trip without the waiting times). Go down a few steps to the Géant glacier, and rope up.
It is also possible to reach the Pointe Helbronner by the cable-car system on the Italian side (in that case go through the Mont-Blanc tunnel).

- **Ascent**: heading north-west, reach the Col des Flambeaux (3407 m). Walk in a south-westerly direction towards the Aiguille de Toule. Close to the Col Oriental de Toule, you reach a short steep snow slope leading to the poorly defined east ridge (possibility of a bergschrund).
Climb the rocky natural steps to the summit, about a hundred metres.
This ridge is often in mixed terrain in the early summer, which, without increasing the difficulty, gives it a noticeably more aesthetic feel.

- **Descent**: follow the same route in reverse.

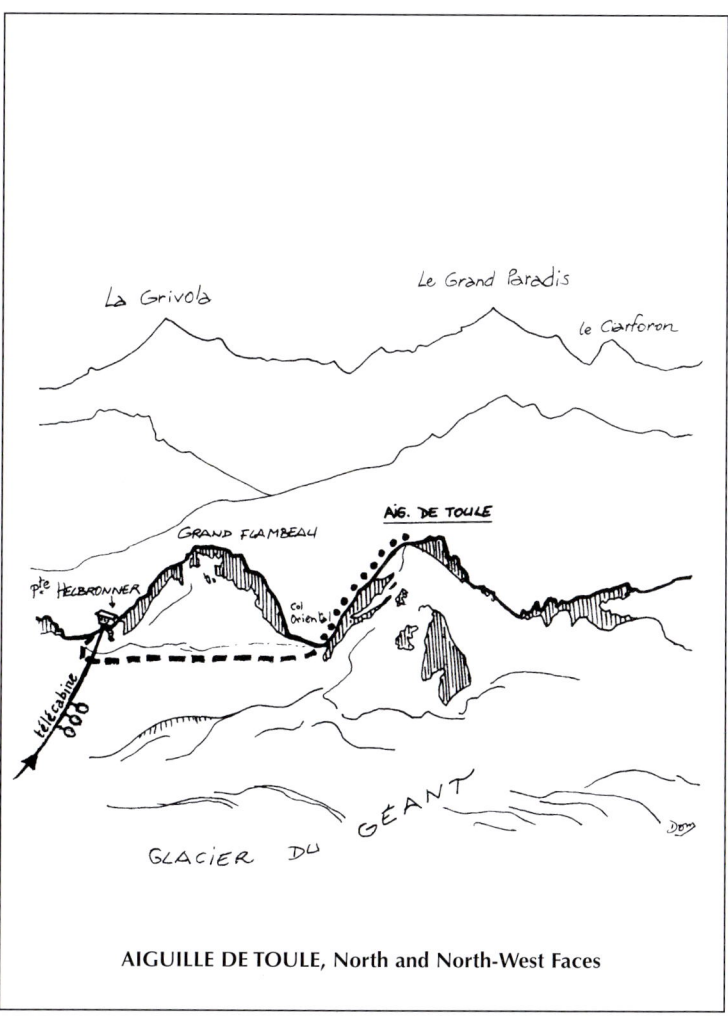

AIGUILLE DE TOULE, North and North-West Faces

AIGUILLE DES GRANDS MONTETS (3297 m)
East Face

As a miniature snow route, this ascent has been selected to familiarise you with the high mountain environment. The surroundings are gorgeous, and the absence of serious commitment, due to the proximity of the cable-car, allows you to venture forth in a more relaxed frame of mind. However, the route is quite high in altitude, over 3000 m, and you will therefore have to meet the challenge of such an environment: a bergschrund to cross, crevasses to get round, a steep snow slope - about 30° - which means that if the conditions are not too good, you may have to climb in "pitches", that is, one at a time.

But rest assured, you will find all these aspects in proportions appropriate to the capacities of novice climbers with only a basic knowledge of mountaineering. However, if you find that the slope is icy, we recommend that novices turn back, as this would necessitate a thorough knowledge of belaying on ice, and crampon techniques.

First ascent: this peak was climbed for the first time in July 1863 by *A.A. Reilly*, with the guides *Henri Charlet* and *Alexander Albrecht.*

Difficulty : Easy (F). The main difficulty lies in crossing both bergschrunds, the one on the Rognons glacier, on the initial descent, and the one which blocks the beginning of the face. At these two points it is wise to belay.
Height : 180 metres, between 3120 m and 3297 m.
Time : allow for about 2 hours to complete the "circuit".
Suitable period : June, July, August.
Equipment : ice-axe, crampons, gloves, sunglasses, rope, harness, warm clothing.
Descente : no problem... from the summit some metal steps just lead you to the cable-car.
Map : I.G.N. TOP 25 3630 OT CHAMONIX

**On the summit slope
Photo: Dominique POTARD**

- **Approach**: this one is downhill - quite rare in the mountains!... But first take both stages of the Grands Montets cable-car, departing from Argentière.
From the top station (alt. 3270 m) go down the metal staircase (about 200 steps...) to the Col des Grands Montets (3223 m). Put on crampons and rope up (about 15 m apart). Walk down a slope, rather steep at first, in a north-eastern direction, and cross the bergschrund. There usually is a good track there, leading to the Argentière Hut. Keep on the track for about 200 m then keep to your left, walking along the foot of the orange-coloured rock-faces on the south-east side of the Aiguille des Grands Montets (a rock climbing venue, rarely used). Skirt left around a large crevasse barring access to the slope underneath the rocks. The rocky ridge gets lower and lower until you can pass onto the east-north-east slope, at the foot of the much coveted face...

- **Ascent**: cross the bergschrund - preferably on the left - and climb the slope, which gets less and less steep as you rise. Gain a small snowy shoulder, then continue uphill pulling to the right on a moderately angled slope which emerges at the summit of the face.
Choose a comfortable spot to take off your crampons for the next quite impressive section: on the north side, follow the ledge equipped with a metal cable leading to the top viewpoint of the Aiguille des Grands Montets. Up there, your sudden appearance out of horrendous precipices into the midst of amazed tourists will create a sensation... don't forget a pen to sign autographs!

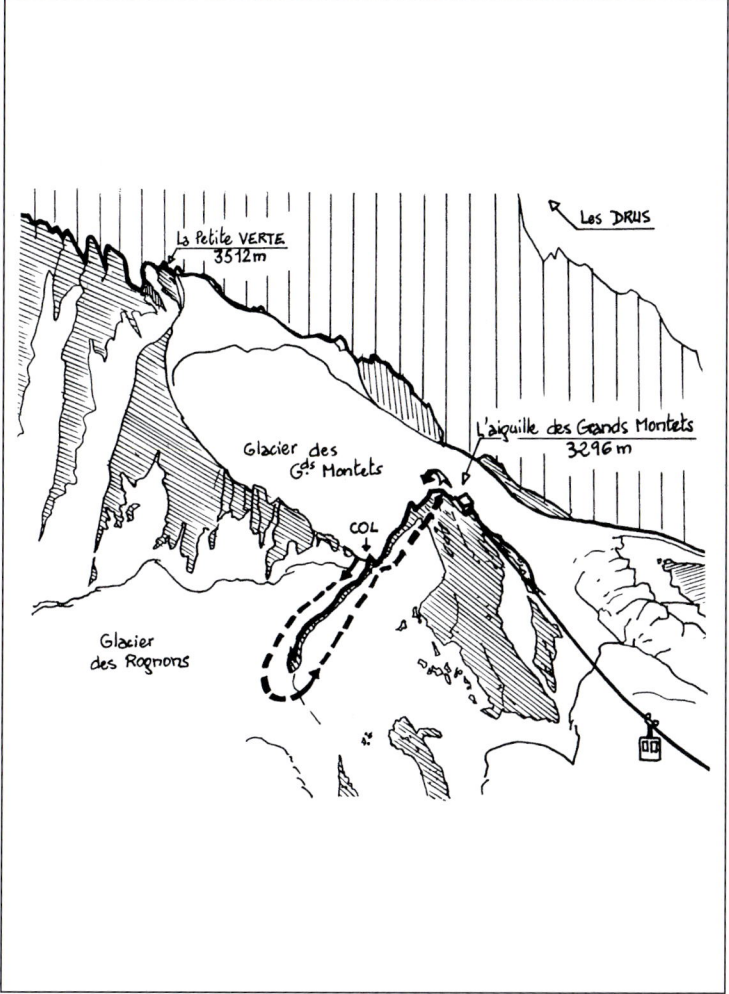

TÊTE BLANCHE (3429 m)
Normal Route

The Dôme de Tête Blanche enables you to reach quite easily the border crest-line going down from the Aiguille du Tour to the Grande Fourche. This easy route, which is entirely on snow, wanders over the vast expanses of the higher part of the Tour glacier. It is a magical place for alpine hiking: vast areas of snow and ice, dizzying light, chiselled rocks. Yield to the spell and enjoy a meditative walk.

The vast Plateau de Trient stretches out on the other side, dominated by many other summits, such as the Aiguilles Dorées (the Golden Peaks). Yet another landscape to discover.

First ascent: *C.H. Russel, R.E. Welbey, and A. Wills with A. Balmat and F. Cachat: 25th August 1857.*

Difficulty : Easy (F): a snow route, to be undertaken only in reliable weather as there is a serious risk in getting lost, in bad weather, on the higher part of the Tour plateau.

Vertical Climb : 1st day: 600 m
: 2nd day: 727 m

Time : 1st day: climb to the Albert Premier Hut: 2h to 2h30
2nd day: Albert Premier Hut to Tête Blanche: 3h

Suitable period : July, August, September.

Equipment : ice-axe, crampons, harness, 30 m rope, 2 ice-screws, glacier glasses, warm clothing, head torch.

Access : from Le Tour village take both stages of the gondola which go to the Col de Balme. On the way down from the route, the track returns to the mid-station, "Charamillon".

Map : I.G.N. TOP 25 3630 OT CHAMONIX

The horizontal ridge of Tête Blanche: the track shows the correct route
Photo: Dominique POTARD

- **Route**:
  1st **day**: Climb to the Albert Premier Hut.
  From the top station of the Balme gondola, follow a good track leading south through a beautiful meadow. The trail turns to the left, overhanging the Tour glacier, then crosses a rocky area, quite steep but easy to climb. Once on the glacial moraine, after an area of big boulders, it goes up the ridge to the hut.

  2nd **day**: the track starts behind the hut, in an easterly direction (locate it the day before). After 15 minutes, you can set foot on the Tour glacier: put on crampons and rope up. Cross it diagonally in an easterly direction, on an even slope, keeping well in line with the Aiguille du Tour. When the slope reaches a first steeper rise, try to identify on your right-hand side a rocky islet called Signal Reilly. Skirt around it on the uphill side, at about 2900 m, to reach gentle, even slopes again. Continue in a south-easterly direction, leaving on your left a first glacial bay leading to the couloir de la Table (don't follow the tracks). Traverse at the bottom of the bowl leading to the Col Supérieur du Tour. Leave the spur descending from it on your left and traverse at the bottom of a second, wider bay, still in the same direction. Tête-Blanche is bordered on its north-west side by a shoulder originating from the Col du Tour. It now becomes clearly visible. (see photograph). Give a wide berth (to the south-east) around the spur and the bergschrund and come back leftwards to the summit, on even slopes.

LA BÉRANGÈRE (3425 m)
Normal Route

La Bérangère overlooks the village of Les Contamines-Montjoie. The traveller to La Bérangère is given the pleasure of contemplating the Tré-la-Tête basin: a high, isolated glacial bastion, surrounded by impressive walls. An unspoilt and wild area which has so far been spared by human development. The Bérangère is the southern extension of the Dômes de Miage, and it is commonly climbed by mountaineers returning from the traverse. But this ascent can be a worthwhile route in its own right, with the climb up the Tré-la-Tête glacier, the snow slopes of the small Bérangère glacier and the rock climb of the final section. An opportunity for would-be alpinists to become familiar with several basic techniques.

First ascent: *Th. Hare, Delphin Fournereaux. August 1858.*

Difficulty	: Easy (F). No technical difficulty on this route. Good physical fitness needed.
Dénivelé	: 1st day: 1450 m / 2nd day: 800 m
Time	: 1st day: 5h to 6h / 2nd day: 3h to 4h / Descent: 4h.
Suitable period	: July, August, September
Equipment	: ice-axe, crampons, 30 m rope, head torch, warm clothing, sunglasses, harness, 2 carabiners, 2 ice screws
Mountain hut	: "Les Conscrits", rebuilt in 1996. Altitude 2600 m, 2 km south of its previous setting. 84 beds. Tel: 04.79.89.09.03
Map	: I.G.N. TOP 25 3531 ET. Saint-Gervais

- **Approach**: park at the hamlet of Cugnon, 300 m on the left after leaving the village of Les Contamines-Montjoie. Follow a track up through a beautiful forest. At the first intersection, turn right and walk on for 1h30 to the "Chalet-Hôtel de Tré-la-Tête (1970 m).

- **Ascent:**
  1ˢᵗ day: from the hotel, follow the track leading to the "mauvais pas" (bad step), a steep section at the end of which you can set foot on the snout of the Tré-la-Tête glacier, covered by scree at that spot. Follow the cairns marking the trail to the ice. Rope up and put on crampons there.
  Walk up the middle of the glacier, skirting round several crevasses. Leave the glacier before a large barrier of seracs, indicated as Tré-la-Grande on the map. Go up the lateral moraine on your left-hand side (right-bank) to try and locate a steep path up the cliff, which leads to the Conscrits Hut in about 1h30.

  2ⁿᵈ day: walk up in a north-easterly direction through the bowl formed at the bottom of the Pointe des Conscrits until you reach a snowy saddle (3200 m). Then, follow the left bank of the small Bérangère glacier, at a short distance from the spur coming down from the summit.
  Climb as high as possible up the steep final snow slopes, then set foot on the rock. Scramble up the final rock section to the summit (4 hours from the hut to the top).

- **Descent:** follow the same route in reverse to the Conscrits and the Contamines. Time: 4 to 5h

AIGUILLE DE LA GLIÈRE (2825 m)
Normal Route

The Aiguilles Rouges Massif is on the "sunny" side of the Chamonix valley. It has always been a privileged place to learn about mountaineering, because it has on a small scale the same type of terrain found in higher places: snow, rock and sometimes ice.

The Aiguille de la Glière is the most accessible summit of the chain: an easy ascent from the Index gondola for a first contact with the world of mountains and, as a bonus, unrestricted and stunning views over the granite mountains of the Mont-blanc range and the limestone foothills.

Difficulty : Easy (F): no major difficulty on this route, apart from route-finding and a wearisome initial walk on the moraine when the snow-cover is poor. An excellent exercise for finding your "mountain feet".

Access : take the Flégère cable-car at Les Praz, then the Index chairlift.

Map : I.G.N. TOP 25 3630 OT CHAMONIX

- **Route**: from the top station of the Index chairlift, walk down in a north-westerly direction on a large neve or scree slope, depending on the snow cover. Try to pick out, on the opposite side, a narrow gully facing east, easily identifiable by a rocky tower, the Gendarme Wehrlin- sticking up in the middle. It is better to reach the base of this gully by first going up a long neve and then the moraine (rope up and put on crampons in the case of hard-packed snow). It is best to approach the gully from the right side at the last minute so as to avoid possible stonefall.

At the foot of the gendarme, step onto a ledge on the left and traverse horizontally to reach a corner that can be climbed easily. Climb it for about 20 meters until you reach another ledge and the summit comes into view. Complete the ascent by walking up a neve (steeper at the end), keeping to your left. All you need to do then is to follow the beautiful summit ridge to the top.

Normal Route of the Aiguille de la Glière

For mountaineers familiar with rock climbing, it is possible to climb the rocky tower bordering the northern part of this ridge: approach it from the south, then pass onto the eastern side. Several moves of 3. Belay using rock spikes and take care to apply the same safety measures on the descent.

- **Descent**: follow the same route in reverse. Beware of crampons "balling up" in the gully!

LE COL DU TOUR NOIR (3535 m)
Argentière Side

One cannot remain unmoved by the "grandeur" of the Argentière basin, an open-air theatre which has witnessed a number of the great acts in the history of Alpinism. There, the phrase "North Face" takes on its true dimension: the tremendous wall, several kilometres wide, stretching from the Dolent to the Aiguille Verte, often called just "La Verte", is one of the most imposing in the Alps.

The Col du Tour Noir sits opposite this gigantic rock-wall and ascending to it in the first rays of dawn, one sometimes witnesses a fascinating sound and light show, produced by the serac-falls!

The route involves no serious difficulty, but it will allow you to perfect your route-finding abilities among crevasses, especially on the Argentière glacier.

First ascent: *H.B. George and R.J.S. MacDonald with the guides Melchior Anderegg and Christian Almer, 22nd July 1863.*

Difficulty	: Easy (F): this route is entirely on glaciers. The most difficult part is the access to (and descent from) the Argentière Hut, due to several heavily crevassed sections, especially at the end of the summer. Make sure you return early enough 2pm at the latest) to catch the last cable-car down from Lognan.
Vertical climb	: about 800 m from the hut.
Suitable period	: June, July, until mid-August.
Equipment	: ice-axe, crampons, harness, 30 m rope, a few ice-screws (just in case), gloves, glacier glasses, warm clothing.
Mountain hut	: wardened all summer. Tel: 04.50.53.16.92
Map	: I.G.N. TOP 25 3630 OT CHAMONIX

The Col du Tour Noir - Photo: Dominique POTARD

- **Approach**: Climb to the Argentière Hut:
  From Chamonix, take the direction of Argentière and take the Grands Montets cable-car to the top station (3297 m). Go down the metal steps to the Col des Grands Montets (3233 m). Rope up and put on crampons (unless the snow is very soft). Heading to the north-east, get onto the Rognons glacier (cross bergschrund) and go down passing just to the right of a small rocky blob (rognon) at the bottom of the first slope (large crevasse). Continue down on a very wide hilltop to the triangulation point (signal géodésique) (3000 m). Head down diagonally to the right towards the Argentière glacier: a "boggy" area in thaw conditions (30 mn).
  Walk diagonally up the gentle slope of this wide glacier, crossing progressively to the left (crevasses) until you reach the base of the curved moraine which surrounds the hut, on the opposite side (40 mn).
  From there, a good track among granite boulders, marked in red, leads up to the Argentière hut (15 mn).

- **Ascent**: Go up the moraine (large boulders) above the hut, following a fairly well-marked trail running alongside a water pipe (locate it the day before). Follow the crest of this moraine to its end, put on crampons and rope up (45 mn). Walk up the Améthystes glacier, keeping to the left. Pass to the left of a first fracture zone on the glacier, more or less obvious depending on conditions, and reach a first false plateau, (3400 m). Make a wide detour to the right to skirt round a moderately crevassed area and reach a second small plateau, below the Col. Reach the Col after crossing a small bergschrund and a short rocky slope (3 hours from the hut).

- **Descent**: follow the same route in reverse.
  Return from the Argentière Hut to Lognan (mid-station of the Grands Montets cable-car):
  Go back down the Argentière glacier by the same route as on the ascent, to the point where the track climbs up towards the Rognons glacier. There, con-

tinue along the Argentière glacier on a long flat stretch - the glacier descends progressively and, choosing the best possible route round the first crevasses, reach a big granite boulder on the left hand-side, marked with a large square of white paint.

Follow the red marks leading diagonally down the moraine. At the bottom of this descent, a ladder gives access back onto the glacier (belay for this tricky section).

Follow the glacier for quite a while, keeping to the left. (the track gets on and off the lateral moraine), then climb a short slope on the left, before the serac-fall. This place is called the "Point de Vue" (viewpoint), (2338 m). Walk down the moraine, then down a steep path going left across grassy slopes, towards the rain gauge. From there, a wide track leads almost horizontally back to Lognan (2h30).

AIGUILLE DU TOUR (3542 m)
Normal Route

The Aiguilles du Tour form the eastern boundary of the Mont-Blanc massif, straddling the French-Swiss border. They open up a new horizon over the Trient glacier and the Valaisian Alps, which seem nearer from here: Grand Combin, Matterhorn, Mont-Rose... the well-known names take on shapes.

The normal route follows the the Tour glacier before moving onto the sunny side of the Trient basin. The last 100 m of pure rock climbing are a great way to end the ascent of this beautiful, distinctive summit.

The ascent of the Aiguille du Tour alone, with its varied landscapes and the different techniques it calls upon, conjures all the emotions mountaineering can offer: a night in a mountain hut, a walk on the glacier by the light of a head torch, the warm contact with the beautiful granite of the summit... it will be a great learning experience for the would-be mountaineer.

First ascent: *C.G. Heathcote with Moritz Andermatten, 18th August 1864.*

Difficulty : Easy (F). The main difficulty is route-finding on the upper part of the the Tour glacier. Ascent only to be undertaken in good and reliable weather conditions. Technical difficulties are modest.

Dénivelé : 1st day: Col de Balme to Albert Premier Hut: 600 m
2nd day: Albert Premier Hut to Aiguille du Tour: 840 m

Time : 1st day: 2h30 / 2nd day: 3 to 4h climbing.

Suitable period : July, August, mid-September.

Access : from the village of Le Tour, take both sections of the lift to the Col de Balme. On the way down, you can also return to the first station, Charamillon.

Map : I.G.N. TOP 25 3630 OT CHAMONIX

The Trient glacier
Photo: François BURNIER

- **Route**:

   1st day: Climb to the Albert Premier Hut.

   From the top station of the Balme gondola, follow a good track leading south through a beautiful meadow. The trail turns to the left, overhanging the Tour glacier, then crosses a rocky area, quite steep but easy to climb. Once on the glacial moraine, after an area of big boulders, it goes up the ridge to the hut.

   2nd day: The track starts behind the hut, in an easterly direction (locate it the day before). After 15 minutes, you can set foot on the Tour glacier: put on crampons and rope up. Cross it diagonally in an easterly direction, on an even slope, keeping well in line with the Aiguille du Tour. When the slope reaches a first steeper rise, try to identify on your right-hand side a rocky islet called Signal Reilly. Skirt around it on the uphill side, at about 2900 m, to reach gentle, even slopes again. Continue in a south-easterly direction, leaving on your left a first glacial bay leading to the Couloir de la Table. Walk up the bowl leading to the Col Supérieur du Tour

   Once on the Trient glacier, head north alongside the Purtscheller ridge. After a steep rise, locate the Tour Peaks (Aiguilles du Tour) and cross the bergschrund situated beneath the gap separating the two peaks. There, a snowy slope leads to wide rocky steps climbing to the gap itself. From the gap, an easy rock climb up the north-east ridge will take you to the south summit.

- **Descent**: follow the same route in reverse.

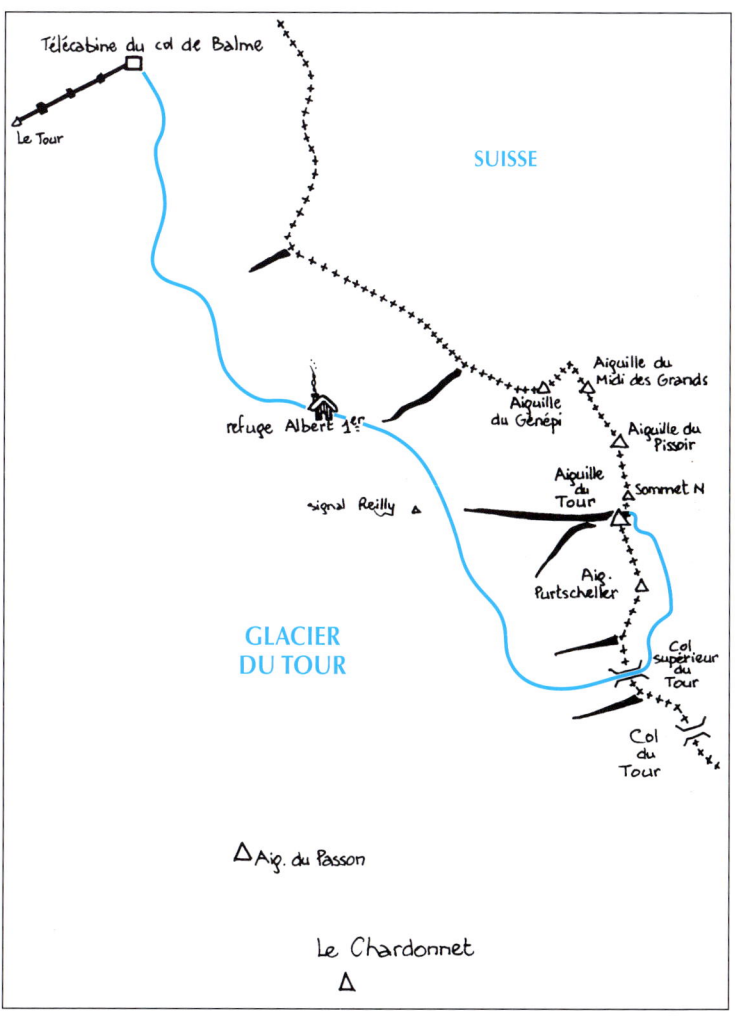

Section three

A SELECTION OF TEN "SLIGHTLY DIFFICULT" ROUTES

1. Le Belvédère . . . . p. 76
2. La Vallée Blanche . . . . p. 80
3. The traverse of the Crochues . . . . p. 83
4. La Petite Verte . . . . p. 88
5. L'Aiguille du Midi . . . . p. 92
6. L'Aiguille de l'M . . . . p. 96
7. The Three Cols . . . . p. 100
8. Le Mont-Blanc du Tacul . . . . p. 106
9. Traverse of the Dômes de Miage . . . . p. 110
10. Le Mont-Blanc . . . . p. 114

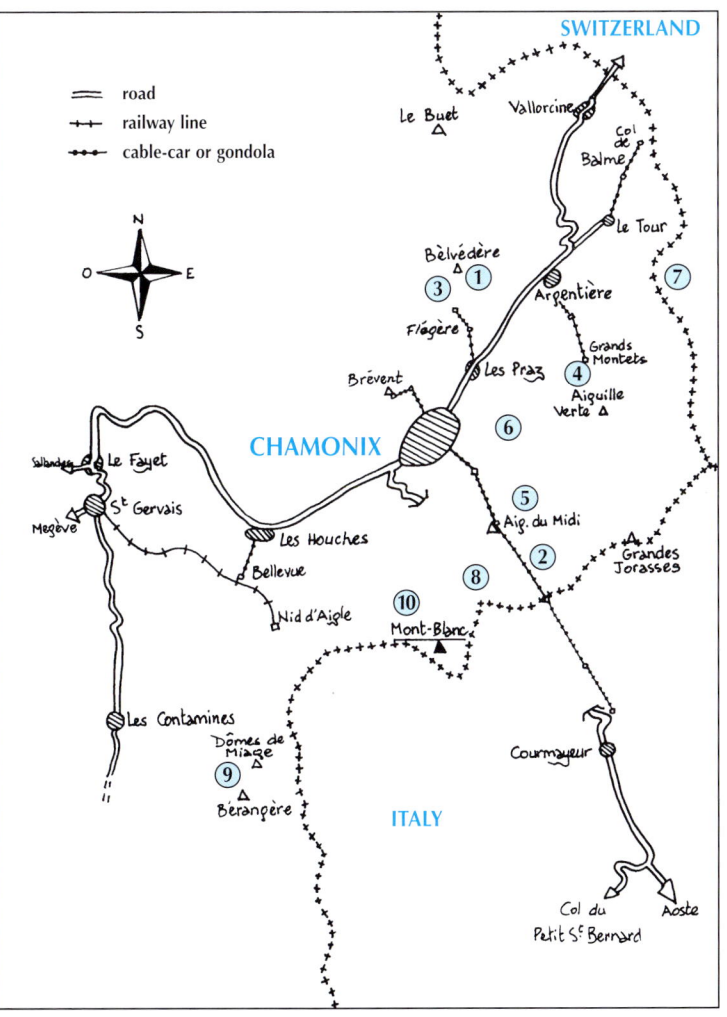

LE BELVEDERE (2965 m)
South Ridge (Normal Route)

This elegant pyramid is the highest point of the Aiguilles Rouges range. Ideally situated opposite the Mont-Blanc Massif, it most certainly deserves its name (the promontory). Topped by a limestone "hat", the Belvédère is a geological curiosity.

The ascent by the normal route was a great classic until an avalanche swept away the Lac Blanc Hut! Then it was less frequented for a while but the hut has now been rebuilt and it makes a comfortable and friendly stop-over. We recommend a night there to have the benefit of sunrise and do the climb in two days. The ascent is made entirely on rock, on a long, fairly even ridge.

First ascent: estimated prior to 1883.

Difficulty : Easy (F). At times, the choice of routes on the ridge can be a problem. A good way to stay on the right route is to rely on signs of passage (absence of lichen, polished rock).

Height : 150 m of actual climbing

Time : gondola to summit 4h30, or in two days:
1st day: Index chairlift to Lac Blanc Hut: 1h30
2nd day: Lac Blanc Hut to Belvédère: 3h

Suitable period : from June to October.

Equipment : ice-axe, about 30 m rope, slings, sunglasses, gloves, warm clothing.

Map : I.G.N. TOP 25 3630 OT CHAMONIX

- **Route**: from Chamonix, go to Les Praz to take the Flégère cable-car and then the Index chairlift (2385 m). From there, an obvious signposted track on the north-east side leads horizontally to the Lac Blanc Hut (2352 m) in just over an hour.

The White Lake (Lac Blanc) and the Belvédère
Photo: Jacques BERNY

Skirt round the first lake on the right and traverse between the two lakes to reach a small, fairly steep, track climbing a scree slope, bordered on the left by a small rocky ridge.

At the top, pull to the right and climb a succession of rolling hills and bowls (tracks). Reach the small glacier descending from the Col des Dards, right under the northern summit of the Aiguilles Crochues. Climb the glacier, still keeping to the right, and reach some broken rocks at the base of the Belvédère, leaving the Col des Dards on your left (2790 m): 1h30.

An obvious way across these rocks leads to a first shoulder (follow the tracks). Cross the shoulder, then a tricky rock-slab on the right to reach a gap at the foot of a chimney, just left of the crest of the ridge, which has a very spiky profile. From this point, it is recommended to use climbing equipment. Climb this chimney (2+/3), protecting yourselves in the higher section using rock spikes (place slings).

Then, climbing by small rises alternating more and more with scree (skirt round a big mound of rocks on its left), reach the northern shoulder of the Belvédère, about 100 m higher.

Continue towards the summit, to a horizontal ledge from which you will get onto a totally different ridge, by traversing entirely the top part of the east face of the Belvédère. This ledge, about 30 m below the summit, leads to the north-east ridge which can easily be scrambled up to the summit (1h30).

- **Descent**: follow the same route in reverse, taking care to protect yourselves in the chimney. The first person to go down places the slings.

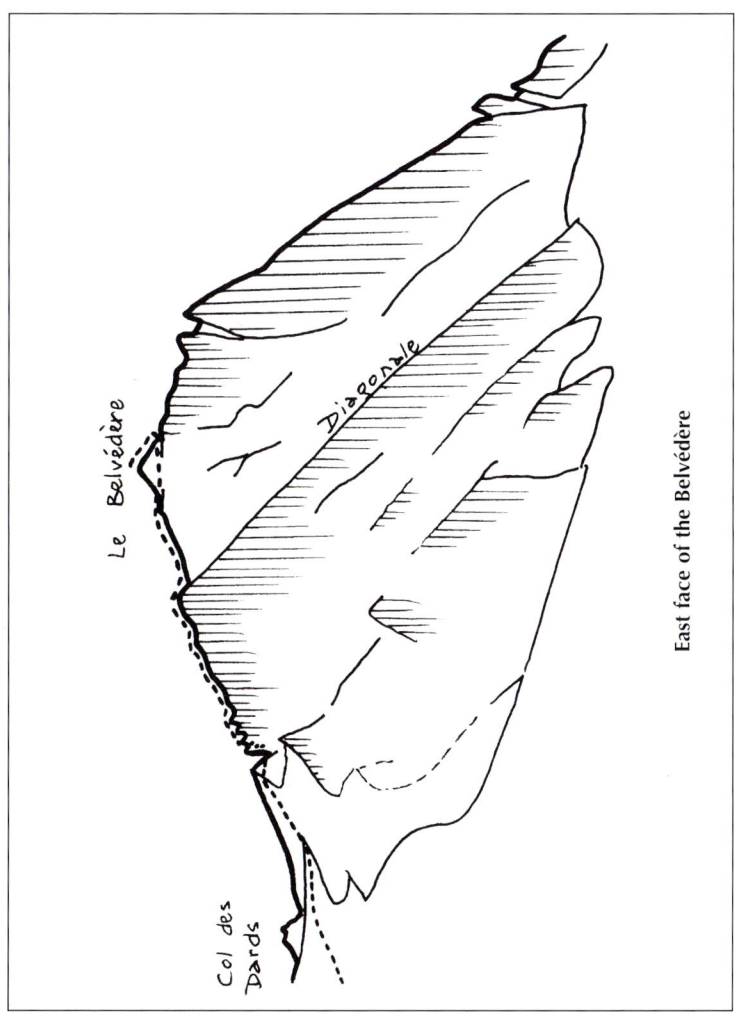

East face of the Belvédère

LA VALLÉE BLANCHE
Traverse

A magnificent glacier walk from the Aiguille du Midi to the Pointe Helbronner, in Italy. The return trip can be taken on the Vallée Blanche gondola. The route is downhill for two thirds of the way, across the high basin pouring forth the famous ice-sea (La Mer de Glace) formed by the Géant glacier. This route is situated in the very heart of the Mont-Blanc Massif.

It will give you a chance to appreciate the full extent of the range, to get close to some prestigious summits and to admire the amazing towers of red granite on the north-east face of Mont-Blanc du Tacul. The traverse does not present any technical difficulties as it is (only!) a walk on a glacier. However be especially wary walking down the arête from the Aiguille du Midi, at the very beginning, as well as when crossing the crevassed passages.

Difficulty : Easy (F). The cable-car goes up to over 3800 m. If you are not in good physical condition, you might feel the effects of altitude.
Route to be undertaken only in reliable weather conditions.

Vertical descent : 650 m

Vertical climb : 350 m

Time : 3 to 4 hours for the traverse plus one hour for the return by gondola.

Suitable period : from July to August (later if the snow cover is very good).

Equipment : crampons, ice-axe, 30 m rope, harness, ice-screws, glacier glasses, warm clothing.

Access : by the Aiguille du Midi cable-car. Reach the south peak of the Aiguille, by taking the left hand tunnel after the footbridge. Come out onto the north-east ridge and get equipped (crampons, rope, etc).

Map : I.G.N. TOP 25 3630 OT CHAMONIX

Climbing towards Helbronner, Grand Capucin in the background
Photo: François BURNIER

- **Route**: go down the arête carefully (the most experienced member of the party at the back). Once on the ledge at the bottom of the ridge, go east and come back in a wide loop (about 200 m), so as to tackle the bergschrund at its weakest point. Then return to the vast basin below the Aiguille du Midi, and pass under the impressive south face (numerous tracks).

Traverse a long plateau leading down to the Col du Gros Rognon (first pass close to the Col du Midi, then carry on alongside the north face of Mont-Blanc du Tacul). From the Col, pick out the general direction for the rest of your route: the Flambeaux pass and the Helbronner Peak. Go down across the vast bowl at the foot of the north-east face of Mont-Blanc du Tacul, keeping rather to the right. When the glacier becomes almost flat (at the base of the Adolphe Rey peak), start on the uphill section of the traverse, which is quite tricky at this point.

Climb a series of slopes broken by numerous crevasses, in a north-easterly direction, until you reach the base of the Aiguille de Toule. Walk up a steep slope towards the Col Oriental de Toule (Eastern Pass of Toule), then go to the left towards the Col des Flambeaux, passing under the cables of the gondola. Reach the Pointe Helbronner by following the eastern slope of the Grand Flambeau.

- **Return**: by gondola and cable-car.

THE TRAVERSE OF THE CROCHUES (2840 m)

The finely chiselled ridge of the Aiguilles Crochues offers very pleasant climbing all along its traverse, with several exposed passages. This is the Aiguilles Rouges Massif but the magical atmosphere of the Mont-Blanc Massif is close at hand and as you always change from one side of the ridge to the other, you visual perspective on the mountains continually opens up. It is mainly a rock ascent, on quite reliable gneiss (although fractured).

The difficulties of the climbing itself do not exceed 3/3+, but the protection possibilities cannot compare with those on a crag, and the safety of the party depends on a good use of the terrain: use of rock spikes and mastery of the technique of ridge climbing, the two party-members always trying to walk on opposite sides of the ridge.

First traverse: *Le Bec and T. de Lépiney, 16th August 1920*

Difficulty	: slightly difficult, (P.D.): the chimney at the start, and the section on the east side, both graded 3, make up the main difficulties.
Height	: 320 m of vertical climb for the approach walk, about 200 m of actual climbing.
Time	: Index - Flégère: 5h.
Suitable period	: from June to October.
Equipment	: harness, 40 m rope, tape slings, 2 or 3 medium-sized chocks (optional), gloves, perhaps one ice-axe for the party at the beginning of the season (for the access gully to the Col des Crochues). If you don't feel at ease on snow, an ice-axe could also be handy on the way down. Helmet advisable.
Map	: I.G.N. TOP 25 3630 OT CHAMONIX

- **Approach:** from Chamonix, take both sections of the Flégère lifts at Les Praz, to the top station. ("Index", 2385 m, 2 stages).

Head north and get onto the Index neve. Climb it diagonally to the right until you reach the base of the south-east buttress of the Grande Floria. Skirt around them to the right in a horizontal traverse, then climb a short scree slope to reach a small shoulder. There, the Col des Crochues can be seen, made up of two deep indentations separated by a small "summit" (20 mn). Continue north and traverse diagonally up, under the east face of the Grande Floria, to reach the foot of the spur issuing from this small "summit".

Climb the slopes leading to the right-hand pass, keeping to the left after the first scree slope (vague track). Continue until you reach the upper third of the slope, then cross a small gully, horizontally to the right, to end up on the right hand-side of a direct line to the pass. Climb a steep slope made of big boulders on this side, then go back to the left, in line with the Col. A fairly steep snow gully leads to a narrow passage, just below the Col. From there: if the snow has melted sufficiently, go through a "letter box" to reach the Col; if not, climb the slabs on the left (2+) moving progressively to the right until you reach the Col (1 hour from the Index).

- **Ascent**: On the other side of the pass, the west side, climb up a short scree slope (vague track), to a diedre–chimney, well on the left of the edge of the ridge. Go up this section for about 40 m (3, 2 pitons) and belay on a rock spike. Above, a small scree slope leads to a platform which you leave by the left hand-side, skirting round a rocky shoulder to come onto the north-west slope. There, two small constrictions, separated by sections among big boulders, lead to a gap in the ridge, to the left of two gendarmes. This is the lowest point of this section of the ridge. Cross this gap (2+) and traverse for 4 or 5 m, on the east side, to stand below a small diedre (clearly visible in the photo on the previous page).

Party on the exposed part of the Arête des Crochues, beyond the small diedre
Photo: Dominique POTARD

You can also get to the base of this gap by following the very edge of the ridge, which you reach from the platform: this is aesthetically more fulfilling but the descent is trickier.

Climb the small diedre, an exposed section of 3+, with usually a piton on the left at the start. You will then find yourself on the very crest of the ridge. Follow it on the left-hand side, belay.

Walk on the crest of the ridge, going through a series of small rises (never difficult) with frequent detours onto the less angled left side of the ridge, until you stand below the central summit of the Crochues (the highest peak), easily reached across big boulders and scree slopes (2840 m): 1h30.

The next part of the ascent is easier: leave the summit following the same route as on the ascent, and then head north after a small gendarme on the ridge, which you climb directly. Follow the long crest-line to the North Peaks (2834 m and 2837 m), skirting left round the steep sections (30 mn).

- **Descent**: from the last summit, get onto the neve by a steep scree slope on the Lac Blanc side. Go down the neve in a straight line, heading right after the first large flat stretch. You reach a wide bowl plunging towards Lac Blanc: start going down it, then head right to reach another, narrower, bowl beyond a hilltop. There, a fairly steep scree slope comes into view, leading down to the lake. Skirt around the lake from the left to reach the Lac Blanc Hut (45 mn). From there, an excellent track leads back south to La Flégère (signposts, 1h15). You can also take the right fork of this track (at the snack-bar), leading to the top of the Index chairlift (longer).

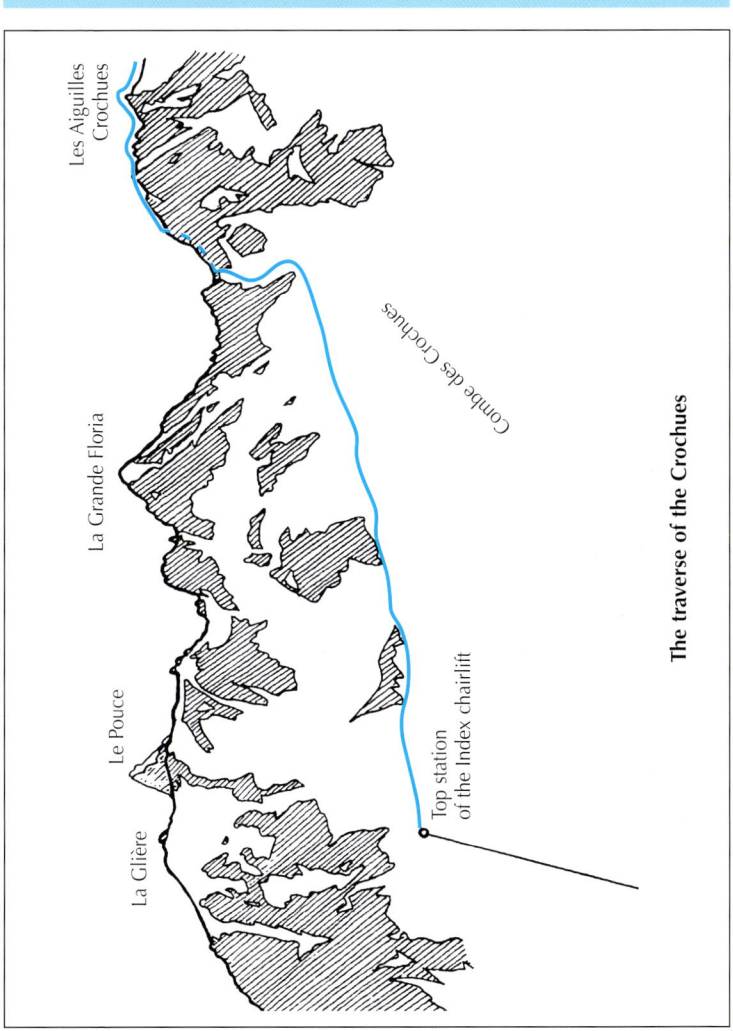

The traverse of the Crochues

PETITE AIGUILLE VERTE (3512 m)
Normal Route

With the construction of the Grands Montets cable-car, the life of the Petite Verte was transformed radically in the Sixties. This shy pyramid, huddling in the shade of its big sister and almost forgotten by mountaineers, very quickly made a name for itself as one of the most pleasant training routes in the valley: a magnificent setting, varied climbing and, only minutes from your car, the overwhelming beauty of being in high mountains... "Stolen" beauty, perhaps? One might have a sense of "cheating".

However, this short ascent has nowadays become a real "classic", and it is still really worth the (small) effort, if only for the stunning views over the North Faces of the Drus and the Verte.

From a technical point of view, don't underestimate the difficulty, even by the north-west ridge (the normal route), especially late in the season, when the snow gives way to ice.

First ascent:
J.E. and R. Charlet with the guide Pierre Charlet in September 1886

Difficulty : slightly difficult (P.D.): the steep, icy slope leading to the shoulder, beneath the summit, should be approached with a lot of care, using rock spikes for protection, even adding some ice-screws.

Height : 270 m of which 150 m of actual rock-climbing.

Time : 1h30 mn.

Suitable period : June, July, mid-August.

Equipment : ice-axe, crampons, 4 or 5 ice-screws, several slings, possibly a few chocks, approximately 30 m rope, gloves, sunglasses, warm clothing (it is a route at a high altitude, and furthermore facing north).

Map : I.G.N. TOP 25 3630 OT CHAMONIX

On the North-West Ridge / Photo: Didier POUDEROUX

- **Route**: from Chamonix, take the road to Switzerland. Just before Argentière, take the Grands Montets cable-car to the top station. Go down the metal steps to the Col des Grands Montets. Rope up and put on crampons.

  Heading south, climb a first slope - beware of the crevasses at the start - to a sort of plateau. Cross it, pulling progressively to the right to cross the bergschrund at its weakest point, far right, between the ridge leading to the Petite Verte and a small shoulder. Above the bergschrund, climb a short but steep slope to a snowy saddle. This is the base of the north-west ridge. Climb it by a first rise, then an easy section to a second rise which constitutes the technical part of the ascent. Climb it:
  - either by skirting round the first rocks on the left and coming progressively back to the right, then moving sideways to the left. Mixed section.
  - or by following the edge of the north face on a fairly steep, exposed slope. This is the best option in good snow conditions (safe steps) but the possibilities of protection are more precarious.

The next part of the ascent is on rock. At the top of the ridge, step over some rocks to reach a short "chimney". Climb it to an escarpment. On the left there is a short rise which you skirt around going up and to the left.
Behind it, an obvious track, among granite boulders, leads to the summit, which is not very distinctive. In fact the Petite Verte is only the first peak on a long ridge leading to the Aiguille Verte (known as the Grands Montets ridge, it is an ascent on a much larger scale, taking roughly twelve hours and with a fairly complex route).

- **Descent**: follow the same route in reverse. Beware of your crampons "balling up" if the snow has softened in the sun.

The Petite Verte seen from the Grands Montets
Photo: Dominique POTARD

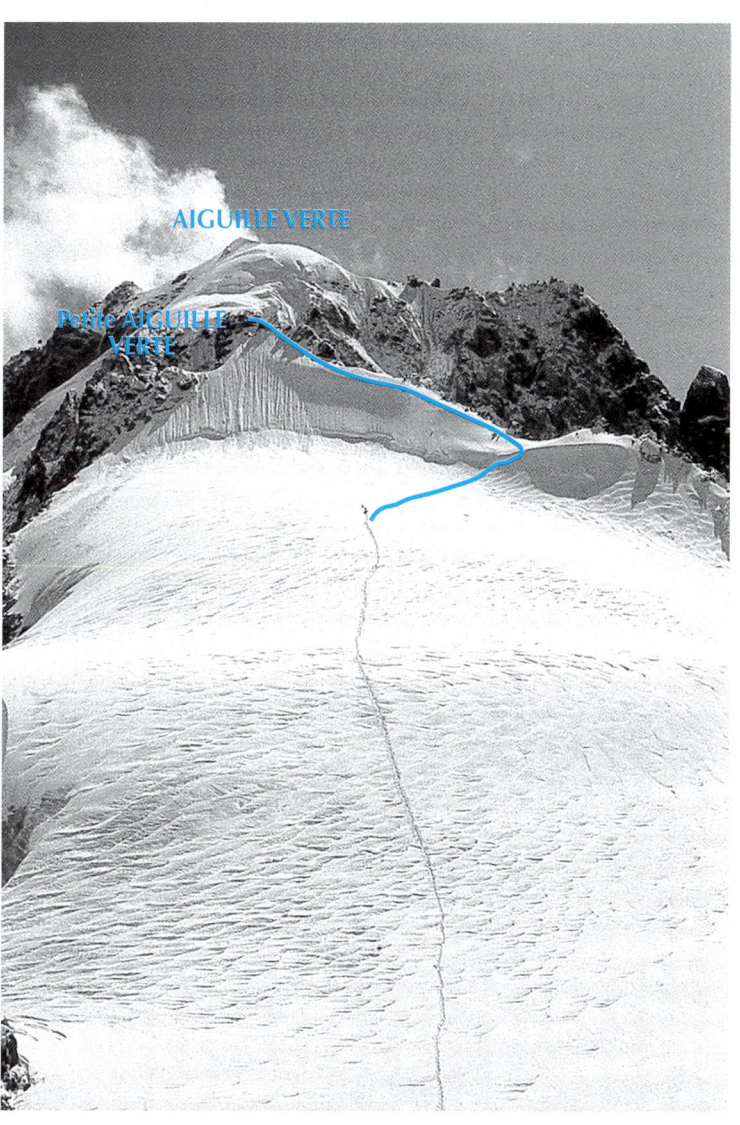

AIGUILLE DU MIDI (3842 m)
Normal Route

The Aiguille du Midi was conquered on the 5th August 1856 by J.A. Devouassoux, A. Simond and J. Simond, three guides hired by the Count de Bouille, a French commanding officer, who financed the expedition.
The exploit was hailed as a triumph and the victorious mountaineers were welcome as heroes by the exulting villagers.
It must be pointed out that even for the most renowned mountaineers of the time, the Aiguille du Midi was seen as an inaccessible summit. It is also one of the few French "firsts" of any scale, stolen from the British, with their untiring appetite for "conquests".
Ironically, this summit, about which the count concluded: "I doubt if there will ever be a second ascent", is now the prey to the assaults of tens of thousands of tourists, both summer and winter... he had not foreseen the cable-car!
The first ascentionists followed a route which climbed for about 20 kms up the largest glacial system in the French Alps, the Mer de Glace and the Géant glacier.
On this two-day trip, in the heart of the massif, you will go through a live geological-science class on the life-cycle of glaciers. It will also be an interesting step in your mountain experience.

First ascent: *A. Simond, J. Simond and J.A. Devouassoux, 5th August 1856*

Difficulty : a long glacier route which requires a good sense of route-finding. Take into account the snow conditions (telephone the Requin Hut for information on the conditions in the Géant seracs).

Vertical climb : 1st day: Montenvers - Requin Hut: 800 m
2nd day: Requin Hut - Aiguille du Midi: 1320 m

Time : 1st day: 3 to 4h - 2nd day: 5 to 6h

Suitable period : July to early August.

Coming out of the Géant seracs - Photo: François BURNIER

Equipment   : ice-axe, crampons, harness, 30 m rope, head torch, 2 ice-screws, 2 carabiners, map, compass, altimeter if possible, glacier glasses, warm clothing.
Access   : by the Montenvers railway.
Map   : I.G.N. TOP 25 3630 OT CHAMONIX

- **Route**:

1st day: climb to the Requin Hut. From the top station, follow a wide track down towards the Mer de Glace ice-cave (do not take the gondola). About a hundred metres after the main track has turned to the left, take a well marked track, signposted "Les Refuges") to the right. Reach a series of metal ladders leading down to the moraine (the access track to the glacier has changed, due to heavy rock-fall, and is now about 100 m below the old track). On the edge of the Mer de Glace, put on rope and crampons. Aim at reaching the middle of the glacier, and climb it, zigzagging through a crevassed area.

An easier section follows: continue up, always keeping to the middle of the glacier. On the right, pick out some ladders, marked by a square of paint, leading to another hut: l'Envers des Aiguilles. Once you are on the same level, just go on, following the curve of the glacier. When the curve becomes more pronounced and the glacier widens (enlarged by the Leschaux glacier), continue up the central section so as to skirt around a crevassed area, on its left. At about 2000 m, when the glacier is flat and easy, pick out the Requin Hut and move towards it. Reach the north side of the spur on which it is built, and climb up to it by a steep track and metal ladders.

2nd day: study the access to the Géant seracs carefully, the day before. Leave the hut by traversing the slope horizontally, in a southerly direction. Cross the next more complex section by walking towards the base of the Petit Rognon, following a vague depression. Once below the Rognon, move back to the left to reach an easier area, marked by a talweg: "la Bédière", the melt-water stream. Follow the side of it, crossing several more crevasses.

At about 2900 m, in the heart of the vast upper basin of the Géant glacier,

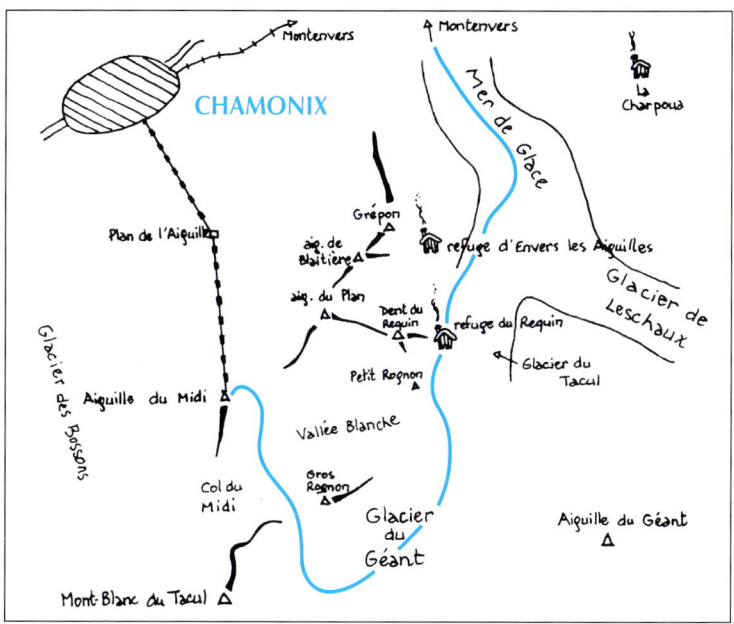

begin a wide loop to the right, passing under the cables of the Vallée Blanche gondola, to reach a wide bowl at the foot of the North-east Face of Mont-Blanc du Tacul. Climb across this bowl to reach the Col du Rognon (3415 m). The Aiguille du Midi can be seen from here. Follow an even slope to the west, at the foot of the North Face of Mont-Blanc du Tacul, then head towards the South Face of the Aiguille du Midi (many tracks).

Skirt round the Aiguille du Midi to the right hand-side, cross a bergschrund and reach the base of the ridge leading up to the peak. Climb up the ridge (very exposed section, crampons essential).

- **Descente**: easy… by cable-car

AIGUILLE DE L'M (2844 m)
Normal Route

> Those peaks, "... whose steep, barren, rocks rise to immense heights, resemble, in a way, buildings in the Gothic style of architecture"
>
> *William WINDHAM, 1741*

The "baby" of the Chamonix Peaks, the Aiguille de l'M owes its name to its shape: it consists of two peaks: the actual Aiguille de l'M and the pointe Albert. Its ascent is one of the great classics of the valley. The astonishing panorama opening up there is exceptional: a plunging view onto the Mer de Glace, the impressive presence of the Grands Charmoz, the Grépon and the Aiguille de Blaitière. The route does require some experience of the mountains, especially on rock, for the final section. Moreover, the ascent is not advisable when the Col de la Bûche couloir is filled with snow, unless you are very familiar with moving on snow.

First ascent: the authors of the "Vallot" guide estimate it prior to before 1856

Difficulty	: slightly difficult, (P.D.): several sections of 3/3+
Height	: 450 m vertical climb to the Col de la Buche, then 60 m of actual rock climbing.
Time	: 3 to 4h.
Suitable period	: mid-July to September.
Equipment	: ice-axe, crampons, (not always essential, depending on the state of the Nantillons glacier), gloves, sunglasses, climbing rope, harness, warm clothing, slings, helmet advisable.
Map	: I.G.N. TOP 25 3630 OT CHAMONIX.

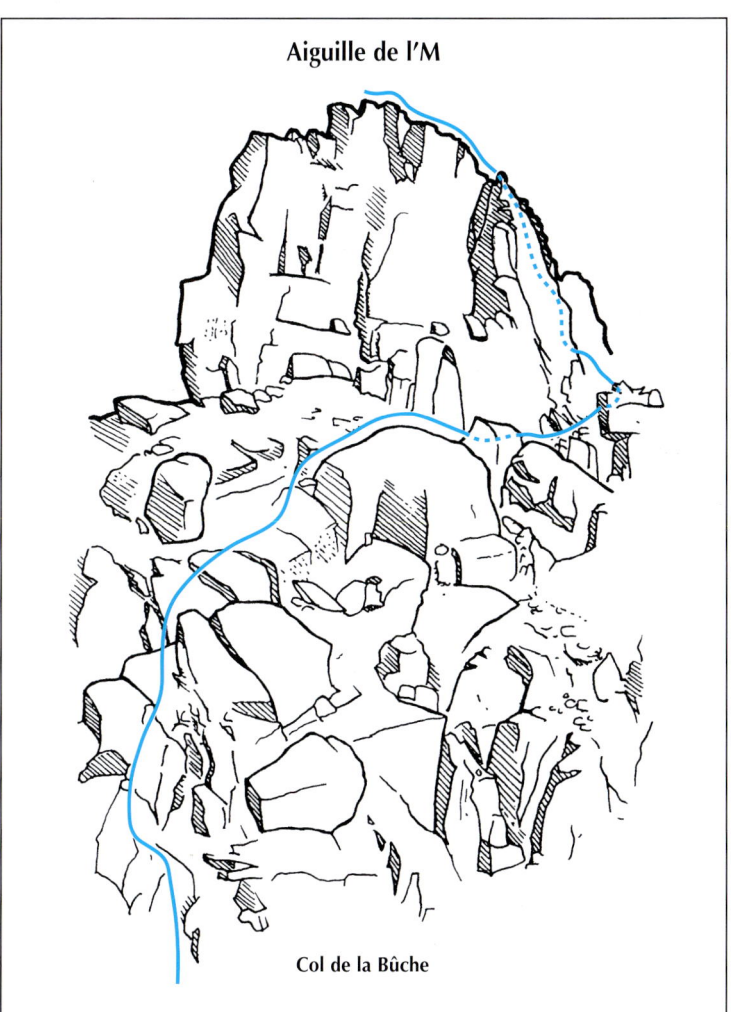

- **Approach**: from the mid-station of the Aiguille du Midi cable-car, called Plan de l'Aiguille, reach the small snack-bar and take the left-hand track towards "Les Nantillons". Pass a little below the Plan de l'Aiguille lake and reach a first moraine. Climb it along a winding track.

  Behind the moraine, traverse horizontally across the slope to the Blaitière glacier which you cross, moving slightly uphill (cairns). The end of this crossing is often tricky due to large unstable boulders. Behind these, reach a small valley, then leave it to climb the steep moraine of the Blaitière. Follow the top of this moraine to a small platform (bivouac site).

  Continue traversing, crossing among big boulders, below a small glacier, to arrive on the Nantillons moraine (track). Rope up and put your helmet on. Climb down onto the Nantillons glacier and cross it quickly (risk of serac falls), until you reach the base of the Col de la Bûche, on the right hand-side. Beware of crevasses (2h) climb the metal ladders then continue up towards the left to cross to the other side of the couloir. Climb broken rocks and steep scree slopes up to the pass: 45 mn.

- **Ascent**: from the Col, get onto a kind of ridge to the left, in a north-westerly direction. A first tricky section, (3+), consisting of a small diedre, leads to a ledge that you must follow, on the right, until you get to a "letter box". Beyond, a series of steps and small walls lead leftwards up to the summit (30 mn).

- **Descent**: follow the same route in reverse.

  Note: this route can also be climbed with an overnight stop at the Plan de l'Aiguille Hut.

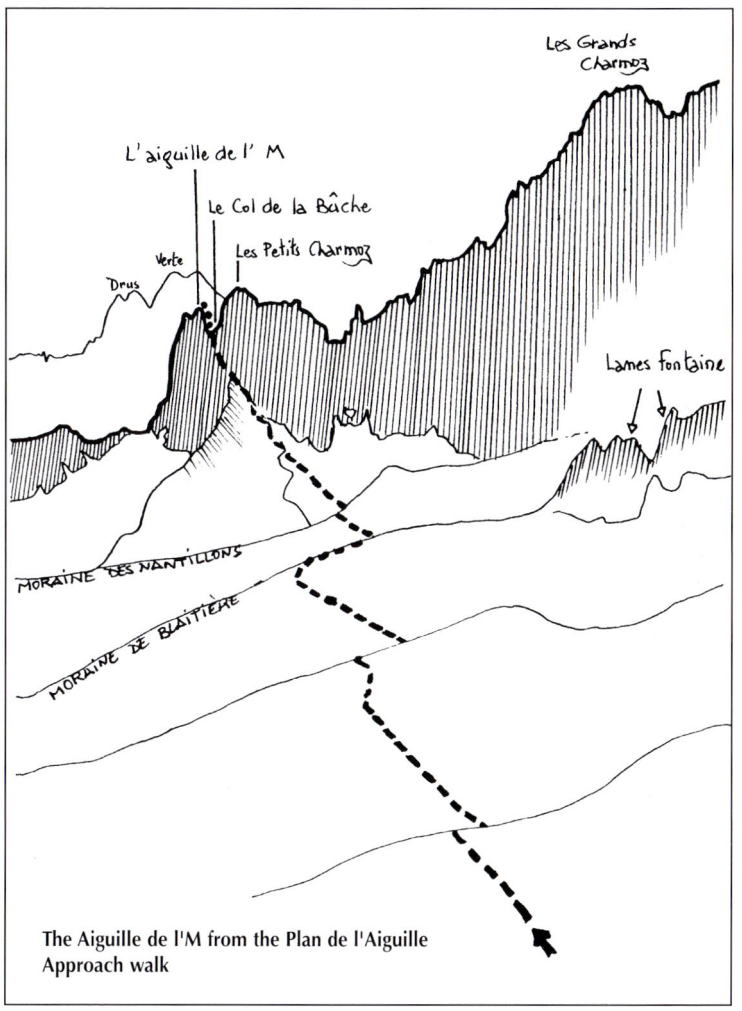

The Aiguille de l'M from the Plan de l'Aiguille Approach walk

THE THREE COLS

The linking of the Col du Tour - Fenêtre de Saleina - Col du Chardonnet is a kind of "cruise" in the high mountains, crossing four magnificent glacial basins and giving you the privilege to discover, in just one trip, the whole northern part of the Mont-Blanc massif. The Chardonnet is followed by the Aiguilles Dorées, then by the Aiguille d'Argentière, with its impressive North Face, along a very aesthetic route, which will definitely appeal to the contemplative mountaineer.

It is a long and exacting route, and to make the most of it, we advise you to spread it over three days, spending nights at the Albert Premier and Argentière Huts.

Difficulty : slightly difficult (P.D.). The main difficulties are the descent of the Fenêtre de Saleina and the ascent of the Col du Chardonnet, both presenting relatively steep snow slopes.

Vertical climb : 1100 m of ascent (the same in descent)

Time : 8h, from hut to hut.

Suitable period : June, July, mid-August.

Equipment : ice-axe, crampons, harness, 30 m rope, several ice-screws, gloves, glacier glasses, warm clothing.

Map : I.G.N. TOP 25 3630 OT CHAMONIX

- **Route**:

  1. Climb to the Albert Premier Hut (2702m):
  From Chamonix go to the village of Le Tour at the far end of the valley (12 km). From there, take the Col de Balme lifts to the top (2 stages). Follow a well-marked track south. After a long ascending traverse, the track goes round a ridge and climbs steeply until it overlooks the Tour glacier. Cross several steep couloirs and reach the moraine, which you climb up to the hut, now clearly visible (2h).

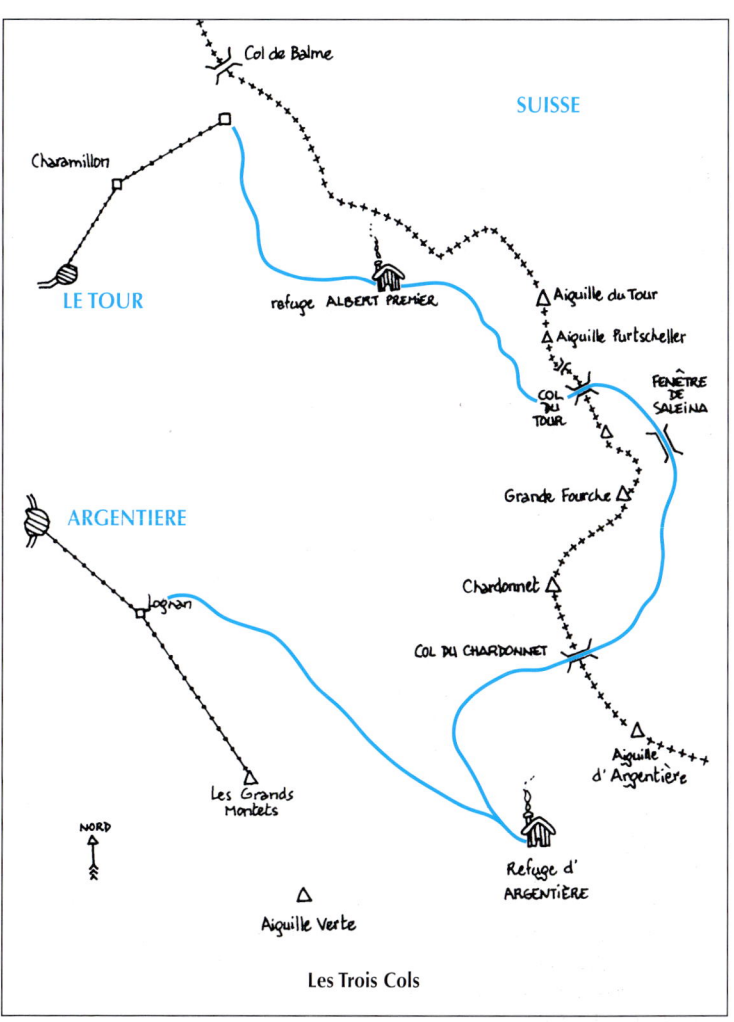

2. Albert Premier Hut - Col du Tour (3282 m)

Follow a vague track across the moraine, starting behind the hut, in a south-easterly direction (pick it out the day before), until you can set foot on the Tour glacier. Rope up and put on crampons (15 mn). Take a curve to the left, and skirt round the Signal Reilly, (2883 m), then climb a first slope, followed by a flat stretch (several crevasses) and a second rise, until you find yourself under the slope rising to the Col Supérieur du Tour.

Leave this track to your left and go on, slowly descending towards the south-east, to skirt round the base of the Aiguilles du Col du Tour. After this, turn in an eastern direction and reach the Col du Tour by a gentle slope (crevasses) after crossing an easy rock section, slightly to the left of the lowest point (2h30 mn).

3. Col du Tour - fenêtre de Saleina (3267 m)

On the other side of the Col, go down a short slope and a small bergschrund and set foot on the Trient glacier. Head in a south-easterly direction, skirting horizontally around the base of the north face of Tête Blanche (White Head) until you reach, on the same level, the fenêtre de Saleina (30 mn).

4. Fenêtre de Saleina - Col du Chardonnet (3323 m)

On easy rock, then by a steep snow slope about 50 m high (rope up), reach the gentle slopes of the Saleina glacier. Follow it first to the south, then progressively turn towards the west. By giving a wide birth around the lower part of the Grande Fourche (Great Fork), reach a position in line with the Col du Chardonnet. It is easy, then, to reach its base (stunning views over the North Face of the Aiguille d'Argentière).

Cross the bergschrund (difficult at times), and, if the snow conditions are good - beginning of the season - climb the steep snow slope directly to the Col, relying more and more on the rocks on the right hand-side.

Later in the season, it may be better to use the right hand-side virtually from the start. Reach it above the bergschrund through a crack, diagonally to the right, for about ten metres, then return left to a wide platform. At the top, a short steep wall (crack) and several easy ledges lead to the Col (2 hours).

5. Col du Chardonnet - Refuge d'Argentière (2771 m)

After the small slope beneath the Col (bergschrund), reach the upper plateau of the Chardonnet glacier by a gentle slope. Bear progressively to the left to get onto the left bank of the glacier, beneath the rocky ridge coming down from the Aiguille d'Argentière. Go down a steeper slope, still keeping to the left, among wide crevasses which call for some zigzagging. Continue diagonally left towards a bowl, directly below the Straton ridge. Walk straight down the bowl until you reach the moraine. From there, a rather steeper track, not well-marked but fairly visible, leads across scree slopes, down to the Argentière glacier. You are then on the lateral moraine on the left bank of the glacier (1h30 mn).

At that point there are two options. You can:
- either go up the moraine, picking the best route round the many crevasses, in a south-south-easterly, then south-easterly, then southerly direction, passing along the whole base of the Aiguille d'Argentière until you reach a moraine shaped in a semi-circle, way beyond the Milieu glacier. The Argentière Hut is about 50 m above this moraine (track marked in red) (1h).
- or cross the Argentière glacier horizontally, in a south-westerly direction, to its left bank (often preferable if late in the season). Join the normal access route to the hut: climb the gentle slope of the glacier, bearing progressively to the left for about a half hour (crevasses), until you reach the right bank of the glacier, at the base of the curved moraine. From there, a good trail marked in red, among large granite boulders, leads to the Argentière Hut (1h15 mn).

6. Argentière Hut - Lognan (1973 m)

Follow the second option (explained above) in reverse, and go down the

Argentière glacier on its left bank to the point where the track climbs back up towards the Rognons glacier.
Continue over a long flat stretch, still on the Argentière glacier, which becomes steeper and steeper. By picking the best route through the first crevasses, reach the moraine on the left bank, on the same level as a large square of white paint on a granite block.
Follow the red marks diagonally down the moraine. At the bottom of the descent, a ladder leads back down to the glacier (belay for this tricky bit). Continue alongside the glacier for quite a while, keeping to the left - the track often uses the lateral moraine. Then, by a short scree slope, climb back up on the left, before the serac-fall, to the crest-ridge of a moraine, called the "Point de Vue" (The Viewpoint), (2338 m).
Go down the moraine, then go to the left on a fairly steep track across grassy slopes, until you get to the rain gauge. From there a wide, almost horizontal track leads back to Lognan (2h30). Make sure you get there before 4.30 pm, to catch the last cable-car down.

Plus jeune ascension du Mont-Blanc:

Youngest person to have ever ascended Mont-Blanc

MONT-BLANC DU TACUL (4248 m)
Normal Route (North-West Face)

The Mont-Blanc du Tacul is a beautiful, classical snow-route, a four-thousander which has become quite accessible and much visited since the building of the Aiguille du Midi cable-car.

At the top, breathtaking views are revealed, especially down the vertiginous Brenva Face, on the Italian side, revealing the architectural dimension and complexity of the whole massif.

4000 meters have always been (and still remain) a symbolic barrier, in the Alpine tradition, above which people call each other "tu", which means that they are on first-name terms regardless of previous acquaintance, age or social status. This is perhaps to signify that in high mountains, a man is simply a man, face to face with nature, and social norms are erased. At 4000 meters, the effects of altitude become more acute: you experience headaches and have trouble breathing. It becomes more difficult to make the necessary efforts. Candidates to the ascent of the "roof of Europe" (Mont-Blanc) will find that the ascent of Mont-Blanc du Tacul is an excellent way to assess their stamina in the new world of very high mountains.

First ascent: *Hudson, Kennedy*, 8th August 1855

Difficulty : slightly difficult,(P.D.): snow route at altitude. Several sections of the north face are exposed to serac-fall.
Vertical climb : about 1000 m, including the climb back to the Aiguille du Midi.
Time : 4 to 5h.
Suitable period : June to September.
Equipment : ice-axe, crampons, harness, 30 m rope, warm clothing, glacier glasses, ice-screws.
Map : I.G.N. TOP 25 3630 OT CHAMONIX
Note : find out about the state of the bergschrund from the O.H.M. in Chamonix.

Going down the great slopes of the Tacul
Photo: François BURNIER

- **Access**: by the Aiguille du Midi cable-car. At the top, head towards the south peak. After the footbridge, take the left hand-side tunnel to come out onto the north-east ridge. Get equipped: rope, crampons, harness.

- **Route**: Go down the ridge carefully. The most experienced member of the party at the back. Once on the small plateau at the bottom of the ridge, make a 200 m loop to the east to cross the bergschrund at its weakest point.
  Traverse below the South Face of the Aiguille du Midi to tackle a long, slightly descending section, leading to the Col du Midi, a vast glacial basin, at the foot of the North-West Face of Mont-Blanc du Tacul.
  Head towards the North Face (there is always a track in summer), aiming for its central section. Walk up a first steep slope until you get to the bergschrund, which you can cross on the right hand-side.
  Once this obstacle has been passed, climb a steep slope, gradually bearing to the right, to reach the shoulder of Mont-Blanc du Tacul, a 500 metre long crest.
  Follow the crest to the east, then south-east, heading towards the rocky part of the summit. You can then reach it by a horizontal traverse on the side of a steep slope facing north (take special care).

- **Descent**: follow the same route in reverse.

Mont-Blanc du Tacul, seen from the Aiguille du Midi
Photo: François BURNIER

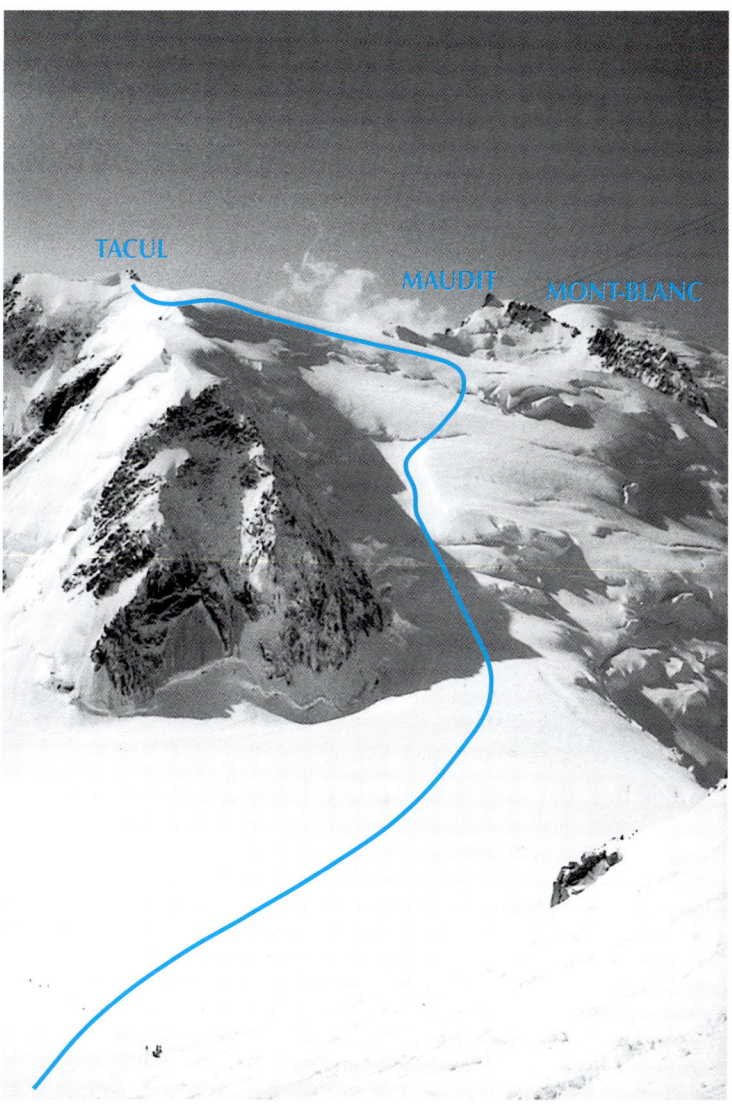

LES DÔMES DE MIAGE (3669 m)
Traverse

The Dômes de Miage dominate the Montjoie valley. They can be identified easily as you drive up the Arve valley. They form a chain of five big humps, closing off the Mont-Blanc massif to the south-west.

The traverse of those snowy summits is one of the few easy ridge routes of such class: unrestricted views over the western slopes of the Massif, totally unspoilt nature and Himalayan perspectives.

Travelling along a slender ridge, sculptured by wind and snow, arouses a strange feeling of exaltation and fear, which is probably due to the constant awareness of the void. Some sections of the traverse call for extreme vigilance at all times. Take special care with the use of crampons (complete mastery essential) and don't tangle your feet up in the rope...

First ascent:
T. Coleman, F. Mollard, and J. Jacquemont, 2nd September 1858

Difficulty : Slightly difficult (P.D). This ascent requires a very good physical condition, because of the significant vertical climb.
It is essential to master the techniques of crampon use and of belaying while moving.
Only undertake the traverse in reliable weather and keep yourself informed about the current snow conditions.

Vertical climb : 1st day: 1600 m.
2nd day: from the Conscrits Hut to the Dôme 3670: 950 m

Time : 1st day: from Le Cugnon to the Conscrits Hut: 5 to 6h.
2nd day: from the hut to the summit of the Bérangère: 5h.
descent: 4 to 5h.

Suitable period : July, August.

Between the second and third Domes
Photo: François BURNIER

Equipment   : ice-axe, crampons, 30 m climbing rope, head-torch, harness, ice-screws, 3 carabiners, warm clothing, glacier glasses.
Map   : I.G.N. TOP 25 3531 ET. Saint-Gervais

- **Approach**: Park at the hamlet of Le Cugnon, 300 m on the left after the village of Les Contamines-Montjoie.
Start on a track going up through a beautiful forest. At a first intersection, turn right and go on for 1h30 to reach the Chalet-Hôtel de Tré-la-Tête (1970 m). Then, follow a track to the east, leading to the area called "le mauvais pas", a steep section, before setting foot on the lower part of the Tré-la-Tête glacier, covered in scree at that spot. Follow a series of cairns up the glacier, until you get to the ice. Rope up and put on crampons. Gradually gain the middle of the glacier in order to avoid the menacing seracs of Tré-la-Grande. At about 2300 m high, before a wide bend in the glacier and another barrier of seracs on the left hand-side, leave the glacier on a track marked by a square of blue paint (perhaps not well-marked nowadays), on the left hand-side (the right bank of the glacier). Follow this track for 1h30 to the Conscrits Hut. Allow 5 to 6 hours for the climb to the hut.

- **Route for the traverse of the Dômes de Miage**: follow an vague track, in a north easterly direction behind the hut, (pick it out the day before), to the Tré-la-Tête glacier (rope, crampons).
First, go north to avoid a heavily crevassed zone by passing above it, then return to the middle of the glacier where it becomes wider and unbroken. Climb the central section, always skirting round obstacles on their right hand-side. About 3300 m high, the slope flattens out and you can identify the Col des Dômes, to the north-west, between the third and fourth Dômes. Reach the bowl leading to the Col from its right bank so as to avoid the seracs. Then climb to the Col by an obvious route. The technical section of the ascent now begins.

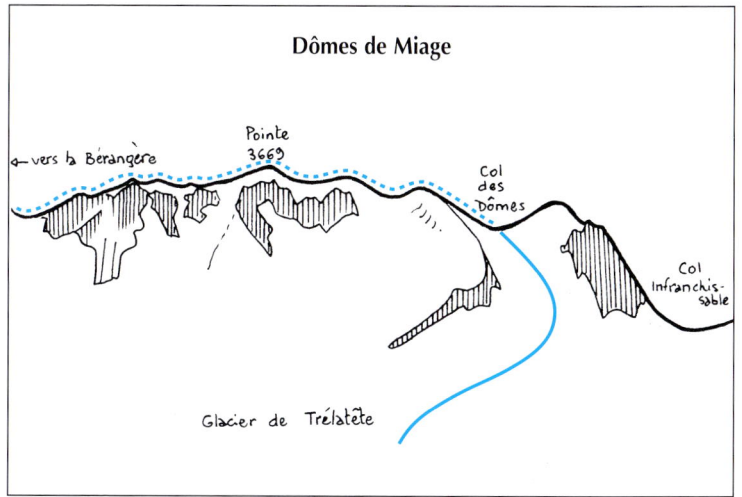

The line of ascent now follow the crest-line in a south-westerly direction until you get to Pointe (3669 m). From there, walk down diagonally, across a series of slopes at the top of the north face, called the Armancette glacier, and reach the Col de la Bérangère.

The descent from the Col to the Tré-la-Tête glacier is difficult. It is better to climb La Bérangère. First, take the ridge climbing from the Col, then, when the ridge becomes too exposed, go up the North Face (ascent on snow or on rock, depending on the conditions).

- **Descent**: follow the south-west ridge of La Bérangère (rock). Climb it down (easy), to get onto a small snow-covered glacier. First, follow it on the left bank, along the rocks. After you reach a flatter area, bear to the right, in a south-westerly direction, and cross a series of long neves (crampons necessary if the snow is hard),and scree slopes (the descent is marked by several cairns) until you get to the track leading back to the Tré-la-Tête glacier or to the Conscrits Hut.

LE MONT-BLANC (4807 m)
Normal Route: Arête des Bosses

Mont-Blanc sits enthroned in the heart of its massif, soaring above all else. No lesser summit can contest its majesty. Its North Face, of simple and massive construction, is framed by the Mont-Maudit Ridge and by the Arête des Bosses, which is the current Normal Route. This face gives birth to the powerful Bossons and Taconnaz glaciers which nearly go down to the bottom of the Chamonix valley. On the Italian side, on the contrary, four major ridges: Peuterey, Innominata, Brouillard, and Bionnassay, make up a complex architecture. As a symbolically significant summit, Mont-Blanc always appeals to the sense of challenge of mountaineers the world over, sooner or later. Whether it is a pursuit for its own sake or a step towards other adventures, the "roof of Europe" remains a permanent challenge, insensitive to trends or fashions.

The story of a conquest

Mont-Blanc was conquered on the 8th August 1786 by Jacques Balmat and Michel-Gabriel Paccard. The original route climbed up by the Montagne de la Côte, the Petit and the Grand Plateau, and reached the summit from the left. Jacques Balmat was a rather poor country-fellow and crystal-hunter from the hamlet of Les Pélerins: "a strapping fellow whose pulse-beat was 46 per minute". Doctor Michel-Gabriel Paccard was a respected Doctor in Medicine, with a passion for "the Sciences" (it was the hey-day of the philosophy of The Enlightenment). The battle for Mont-Blanc was finally won by these two outsiders, after a long series of attempts dating back to 1760, when Monsieur de Saussure, an aristocrat from Geneva, had stuck notices in "Chamouny", offering a reward to anyone who could reach the highest point in Europe.

For the rest of their lives, Paccard and Balmat would quarrel over the mediatic outcome of their first ascent, unable to settle the discussion over who was the first one on the summit... Mountaineering was born on that day of August 1786, bringing out the best and the worst in men.

The top of Mont-Blanc - Photo: François BURNIER

First ascent: by the Arête des Bosses: Leslie Stephen, F. F. Tuckett, Melchior Anderegg, Johan Josef Bennen, 18th July 1861

Difficulty : slightly difficult (P.D.). The first stage of the route, leading to the Goûter Hut, includes the crossing of a very exposed couloir (stonefall). It is the most lethal spot in the whole massif. Moreover, the high altitude at the Goûter Hut (3817 m) can cause significant physiological problems (mountain-sickness). A thorough preparation including other high routes and a time of acclimatisation is essential.

The second stage, from the hut to the summit, should only be undertaken when weather conditions are absolutely reliable. It requires a lot of experience to be able to confront bad weather at such height, and on vast areas of snow with no real landmarks. The narrow and often congested summit ridge requires constant vigilance, which is not always easy when the effects of altitude and tiredness are felt.

Descent : it is important to remain very careful, especially if the snow is hard. If planning to go down via the Grands Mulets, find out about the state of the glacier at the Jonction: that section can be particularly difficult, even impassable. On that route, two sections present objective dangers:
- the Petit Plateau (serac-fall).
- the traverse below the Aiguille du Midi (rock-fall).

Vertical climb : Nid d'Aigle - Goûter Hut, 1400 m
Goûter Hut - Mont-Blanc, 950 m

Time : Nid d'Aigle - Goûter Hut: 4 to 5h, the same from the hut to the summit

Equipment   : ice-axe, crampons, 30 m rope, several ice-screws, harness, warm gloves, glacier glasses, very warm clothing, helmet. Plastic shell boots are highly recommended (or overboots).

Suitable period : mid-June to end of August.

Access   : - either take the Mont-Blanc Tramway (TMB) at the train-station (SNCF) in Le Fayet/Saint-Gervais, to reach Le Nid d'Aigle.
- or take the Bellevue cable-car from the village of Les Houches, then the TMB to Le Nid d'Aigle. TMB: 4 or 5 trains per day. Tel 04.50.78.27.23. Bellevue cable-car: Tel 04.50.54.40.32

- **Route:**

1st day: climb to the Goûter Hut. From the Nid d'Aigle follow a well-trodden track alongside the Montagne des Rognes. At the forestry hut (2768 m, 1h), follow a ridge to the right (marked), leading to the small Tête Rousse glacier (Tête Rousse Hut at 3167 m, 1h). Climb this glacier to the east until you get to a ridge running along the right bank of the couloir coming down from the Aiguille du Goûter. Cross the couloir horizontally when it seems right, watching out for stonefall. If the couloir is snow-covered or icy, use the cable to belay during the traverse. Then, climb a spur of unstable rock marked with red dots, leading to the hut (2 to 3 hours).

2nd day: Goûter Hut to Mont-Blanc. Go up the slope behind the hut to get onto the Aiguille du Goûter. Follow the crest-line to the south-east. A short slope leads up to the foot of the North-West Face of the Dôme du Goûter. Walk up several long and fairly steep slopes, skirting round several serac barriers (usually on the left). Around 4250 m, cross to the left and go over a snowy saddle onto the north-east side of the Dôme. A descending traverse to the south-east leads to the Col du Dôme.(4237 m, 2 hours to 2h30 mn). Pass to the right of the small Vallot Hut, (4362 m, radio beacon) and gain the Grande Bosse Ridge (Great Bump, 4513 m) across some fairly steep slopes. The Petite Bosse follows (Small Bump, 4547 m), then the rocks of La Tournette which you skirt around on their left hand-side. The ridge becomes gradually narrower until you finally get to the summit of Mont-Blanc (4810 m, 2h to 2h30 mn from the Col du Dôme).

- **Descent**:
  - either follow the same route in reverse, which is the easiest. The high risk of rock-fall calls for great care to be taken on the descent from the Goûter Hut, particularly when crossing the large couloir, (4 to 5 hours to Le Nid d'Aigle).
  - or take the Grands Mulets route, which is safer in bad weather. This route returns to the mid-station of the Aiguille du Midi cable-car (Le Plan de l'Aiguille). At the Col du Dôme, turn right to go down towards the Grand Plateau across wide slopes ending in a bowl. Progressively move back to the left (not too far, however, because of numerous crevasses) and reach the Petit Plateau across a steeper slope.

This section is very exposed to serac-falls. A steeper slope, La Côte du Cerisier (the Cherry-tree slope) is followed by a rather heavily crevassed section. Cross them by bearing to the left, then well to the right at the end, to reach the foot of the small rocky spur on which the Grands Mulets Hut stands (3051m) Then walk down a large slope leading to La Jonction, which you leave by bearing progressively to the right (many crevasses) until you reach Plan Glacier, the wide glacial plateau of the Bossons glacier. Cross the glacier in a north-westerly direction to reach its right bank.

Leave the glacier and walk up towards the Gare des Glaciers, across a succession of couloirs where rock-fall is frequent, especially when the sun is on the upper slope. A horizontal track below the Aiguille du Midi leads to the

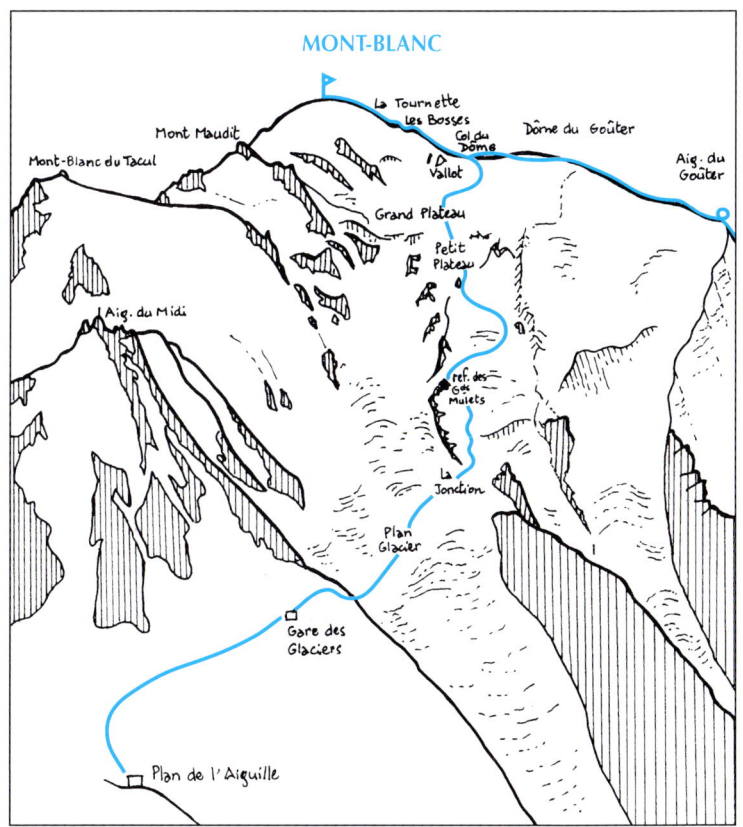

Pélerins glacier, which is reached by crossing an awkward moraine. Cross the glacier horizontally to the right bank moraine. From there, you can easily get to the cable-car station of the Plan de l'Aiguille, (2310 m, count 5 hours from Mont-Blanc). Plan to be there before 5 p.m. to be sure of catching the last car down.

CONTENTS

- Foreword . . . . p. 3

Section one:
an introduction to the technical aspects of mountaineering

- Is it necessary to hire a guide? . . . . p. 8
- Some vocabulary . . . . p. 10
- Equipment and gear . . . . p. 12
- Techniques and safety . . . . p. 16
  - Environmental dangers
  - Route-finding in the mountain
  - Effort at high altitudes
  - Methods of progression
- About the weather . . . . p. 28
- What to do in the event of an accident? . . . . . . p. 29
- Mountain huts . . . . p. 32
- Choosing an ascent and finding information . . . . p. 34
- Knowing when to turn back . . . . p. 37

Section two:
ten easy routes

- Le Buet, normal route . . . . p. 42
- Le Moulin de la Mer de Glace . . . . p. 44
- Le Petit Mont-Blanc . . . . p. 46
- L'Aiguille de Toule, normal route . . . . p. 48

- L'Aiguille des Grands Montets, east face . . . . p. 52
- La Tête Blanche, normal route . . . . p. 56
- La Bérangère, normal route . . . . p. 59
- La Glière, normal route . . . . p. 61
- Le Col du Tour Noir, Argentière side . . . . p. 64
- L'Aiguille du Tour, normal route . . . . p. 68

Section three:
ten slightly difficult routes

- Le Belvédère, normal route . . . . p. 76
- La Vallée Blanche, traverse . . . . p. 80
- Les Aiguilles Crochues, traverse . . . . p. 83
- La Petite Aiguille Verte, normal route . . . . p. 88
- L'Aiguille du Midi, normal route . . . . p. 92
- L'Aiguille de l'M, normal route . . . . p. 96
- The three Cols . . . . p. 100
- Le Mont-Blanc du Tacul, normal route . . . . p. 106
- Les Dômes de Miage, traverse . . . . p. 110
- Le Mont-Blanc, normal route . . . . p. 114

LIST OF ROUTES IN ALPHABETICAL ORDER

- Belvédère (Aiguille du), normal route . . . . p. 76
- Bérangère (Aiguille de la), normal route . . . . . . p. 59
- Buet (Mont), normal route . . . . p. 42
- Crochues (Aiguilles), traverse . . . . p. 83
- Glière (Aiguille de la), normal route . . . . . . p. 61
- Grands Montets (Aiguille des), east face . . . . . p. 52
- M (Aiguille de l'), normal route . . . . p. 96
- Miage (Dômes de), traverse . . . . p. 110
- Midi (Aiguille du), normal route . . . . p. 92
- Mont-Blanc, normal route . . . . p. 114
- Moulin de la Mer de Glace . . . . p. 44
- Petit Mont-Blanc, normal route . . . . p. 46
- Petite Aiguille Verte, normal route . . . . . . p. 88
- Tacul (Mont-Blanc du), normal route . . . . . . p. 106
- Tête Blanche, normal route . . . . p. 56
- The Three Cols . . . . p. 100
- Toule (Aiguille de), normal route . . . . p. 48
- Tour (Aiguille du), normal route . . . . p. 68
- Tour Noir (Col du), Argentière side . . . . . . p. 64
- Vallée Blanche, traverse . . . . p. 80

GLOSSARY OF MOUNTAINEERING TERMS

above	en-haut
abseil	rappel
anchor point	point d'ancrage
ascender	bloqueur mécanique
avalanche transceiver	Arva
balling up	botter
bank (right/left)	rive gauche/droite
belay	assurer
below	en bas
bergschrund	rimaye
boots	chaussures
boulder	bloc
cabin	cabane
cable-car	téléphérique
camming device	bloqueur
carabiner	mousqueton
cap	casquette
chock/stopper	coinceur
climb	ascension
climbing venue	école d'escalade
cornice	corniche
crampons	crampons
crevasse	crevasse
downhill	en aval
figure 8 / belay device	descendeur
flat tape	sangle
fog	brouillard
friction knot	nœud Machard
friend	friend
go round	faire le tour
gondola	télécabine
gully	couloir
hat	chapeau, bonnet
harness	baudrier
helmet	casque
ice	glace
ice-axe	piolet
ice-screw	broche à glace
jacket	veste
left	gauche
lightning	foudre
locking (carabiner)	de sécurité
loop of rope	anneau de corde
loose rock	rocher délité
map	carte
moraine	moraine
mountain-hut	refuge
pass	col
peak	pic/aiguille
pitch	longueur
quick-draw	dégaine
ridge	arête
right	droite
rock	rocher
rock-fall	chute de pierre
rope up	s'encorder

rope	corde
rope/party	cordée
rucksack	sac à dos
scree	éboulis
screwgate	à vis
serac-fall	chute de serac
signpost	panneau
signposted	indiqué
sling	anneau de sangle
slope, side	pente, versant
snow	neige
spike	becquet
storm	orage
top rope	moulinette
top/summit	sommet
track	sentier, trace
trail	piste
uphill	en amont
vertical height	dénivellation
wall	mur
watch out	attention
weather forecast	météo
windslab	plaque à vent

NOTES

NOTES

NOTES

NOTES